DARK STOCK PHOTOS

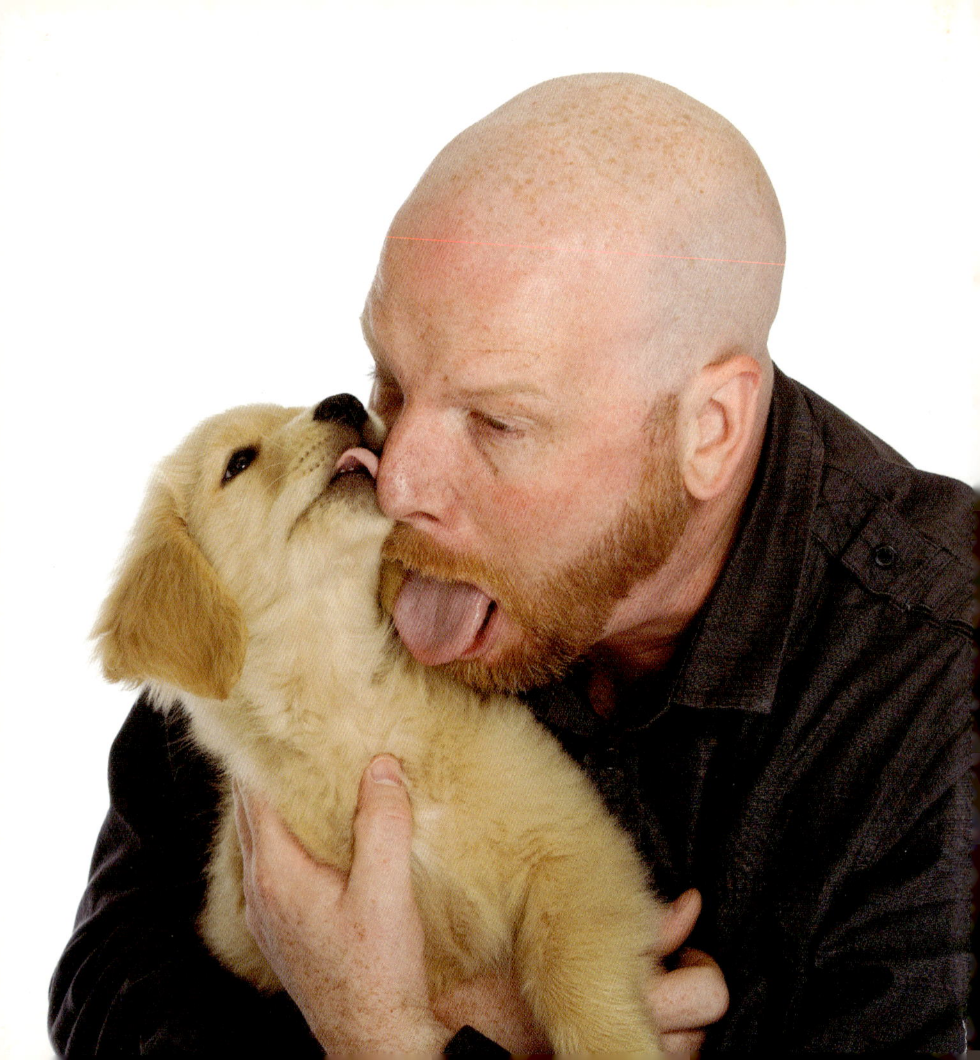

THE VERY BEST OF DARK STOCK PHOTOS

F*CKED UP PHOTOGRAPHY FOR A MESSED UP WORLD

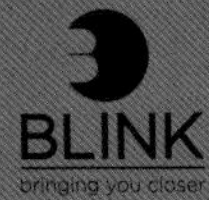

BLINK
bringing you closer

Published by Blink Publishing
2.25, The Plaza,
535 Kings Road,
Chelsea Harbour,
London, SW10 0SZ

www.blinkpublishing.co.uk

facebook.com/blinkpublishing
twitter.com/blinkpublishing

Hardback – 978-1-78870-005-4
Ebook – 978-1-78870-006-1

A CIP catalogue of this book is available from the British Library.

Typset by Envy Limited
Printed and bound in Italy

1 3 5 7 9 10 8 6 4 2

Blink Publishing is an imprint of Bonnier Books UK
www.bonnierbooks.co.uk

INTRODUCTION

A girl smiles and poses for a selfie with an AK-47 slung over her shoulder. A topless man in a Santa hat tweaks his nipples. A doctor lights a cigarette for a sick patient. These are just a few of the bizarre images I found for sale in the dingy, forgotten corners of stock photography websites. But who would ever buy them? And for what purpose? It's a mystery that led me to create Dark Stock Photos, an archive of the weirdest, funniest and most inexplicable stock images being sold on the web.

Most stock photos are unremarkable: grinning businessmen shaking hands in front of flip charts; women laughing and eating salad. They're the kind of banal images you see illustrating corporate brochures and adverts in local papers. And I've always found them hilarious. Models with perfect teeth and fake smiles; cheap sets and flat unflattering lighting: there's an artifice to these images that means they could never, ever be mistaken for reality, like an alien's approximation of the human experience.

But as I explored the cavernous depths of these websites, I noticed images that were… different. I unearthed sinister scenes of depression, suicide, murder, and drug abuse, but skewed by the surreal lens of the stock photographer. And the artless, totally unsubtle presentation of these images make otherwise serious subject matter darkly comic. Seasonal depression is not funny, but a man sitting in front of a Christmas tree with a bottle of whisky in one hand and a gun in the other is. It's so absurdly on the nose that you can't help but laugh.

In one image claiming to illustrate the dangers of drunk driving, a man in a car nonchalantly offers you, his passenger, an open bottle of beer as he skids horizontally across a busy motorway. In another, whose premise is probably a mystery even to the photographer, a man sits on a toilet, screaming, caught up in a whirlwind of toilet paper. And if you ever need a photo of a girl preparing to gulp down a pint of bleach, well, the wonderful world of stock photography has you covered.

And so my obsession began, trawling stock photo galleries for the strangest, bleakest images I could find. This led to the creation of Dark Stock Photos, a Twitter account that somehow managed to amass over 200,000 followers in a just a few months. It was reassuring to discover that people were just as baffled, intrigued and beguiled by these insane images as me, and it encouraged me to dive deeper, search harder, and really try to disturb people. And the tome you're holding in your hands right now is the result of that dark quest. Apologies in advance.

Andy Kelly, August 2018

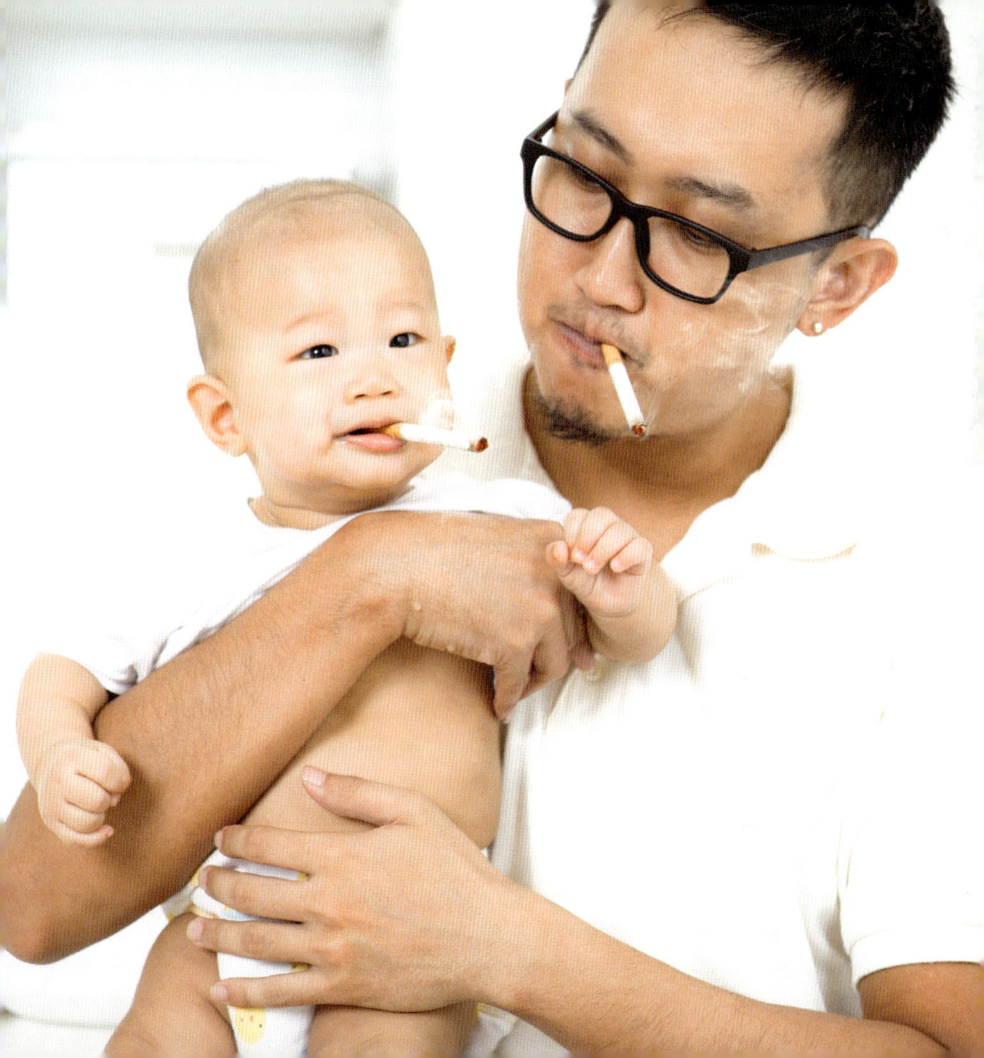

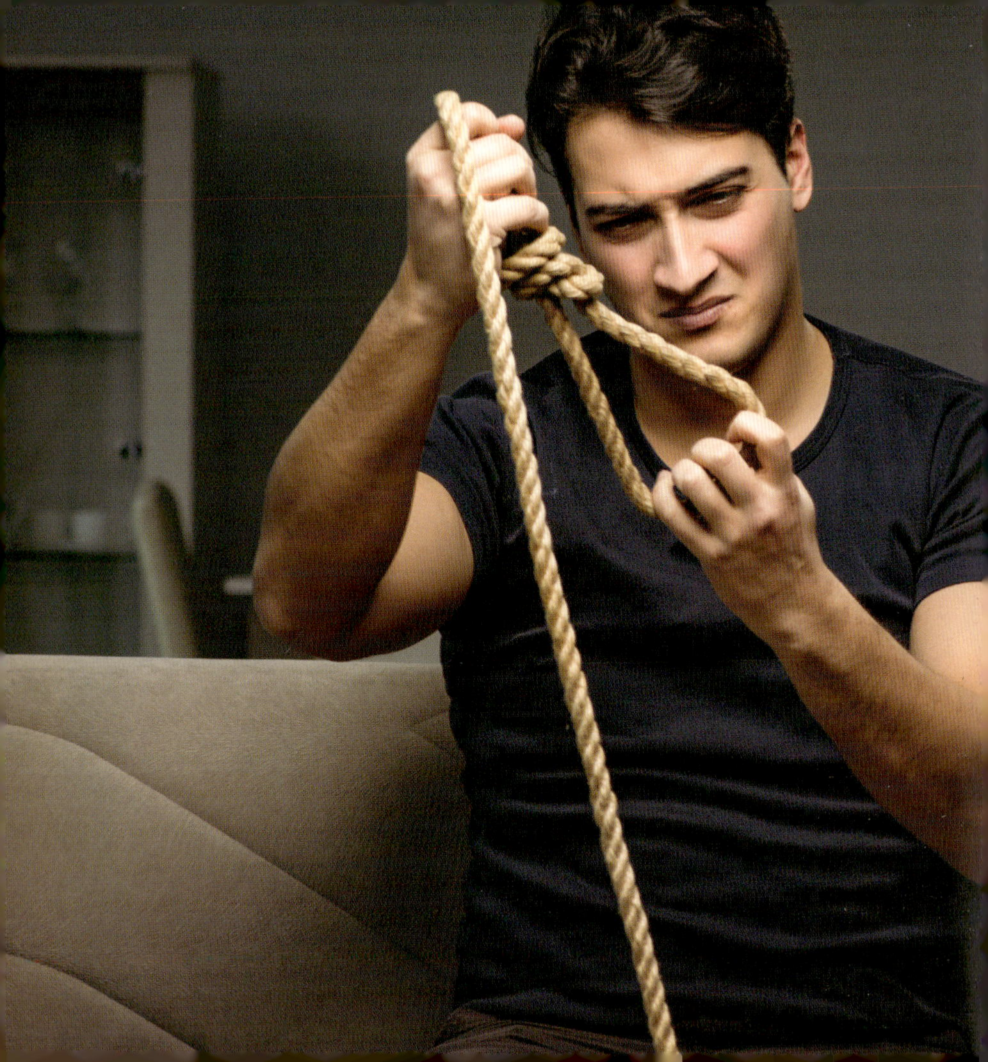

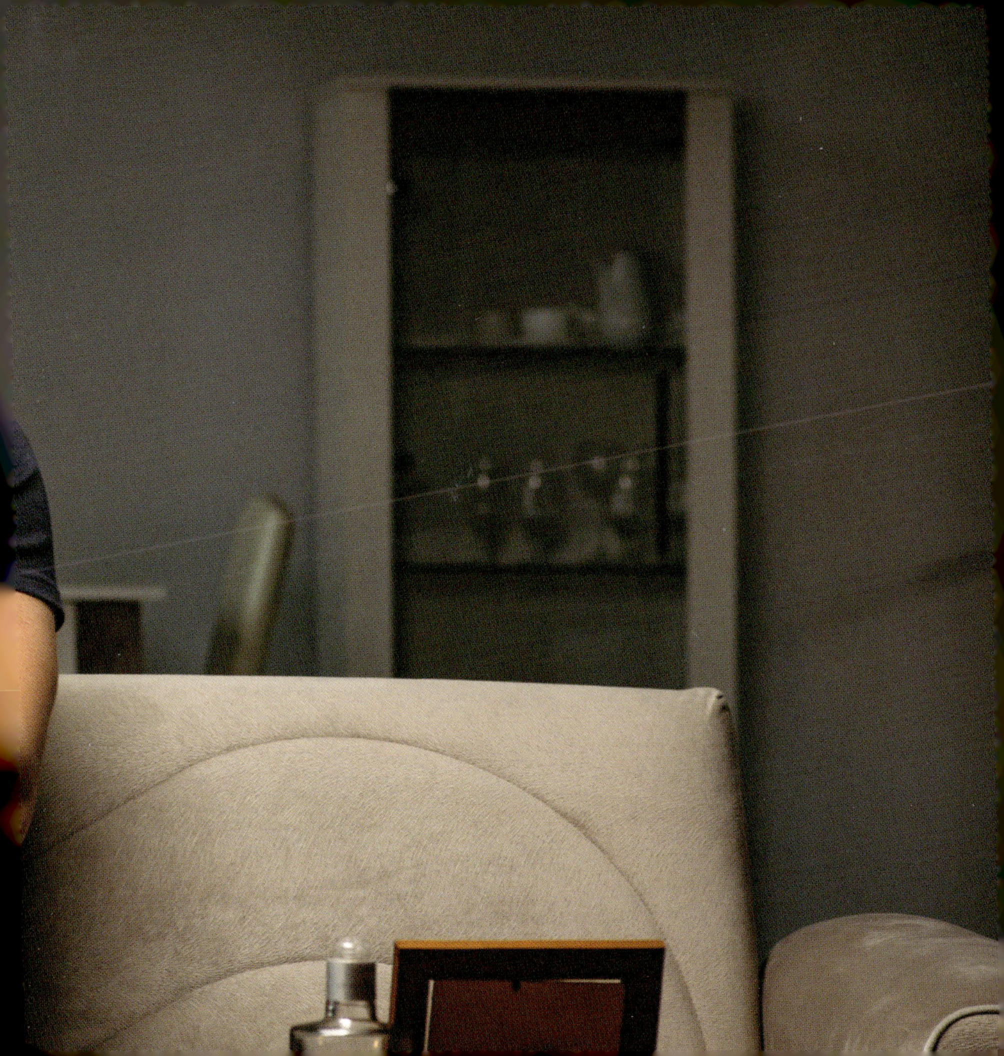

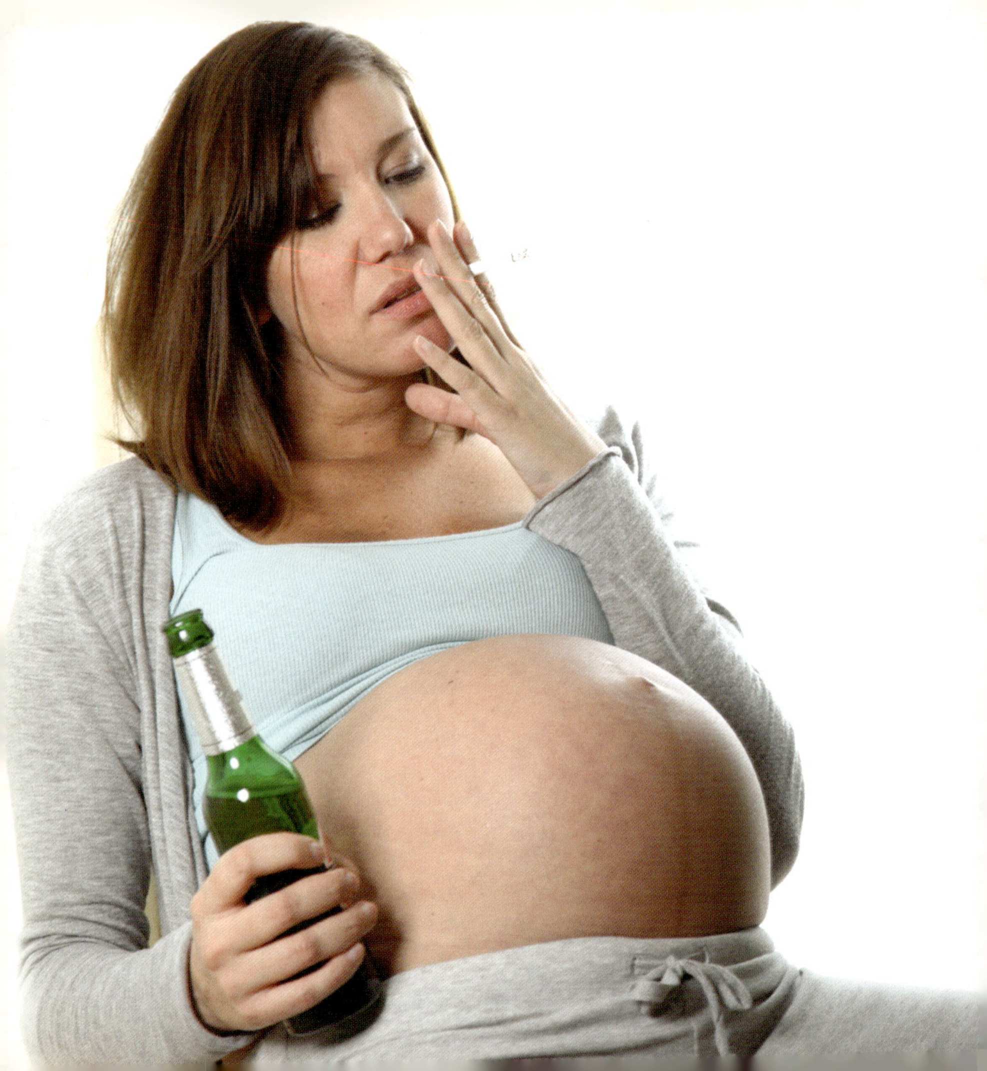

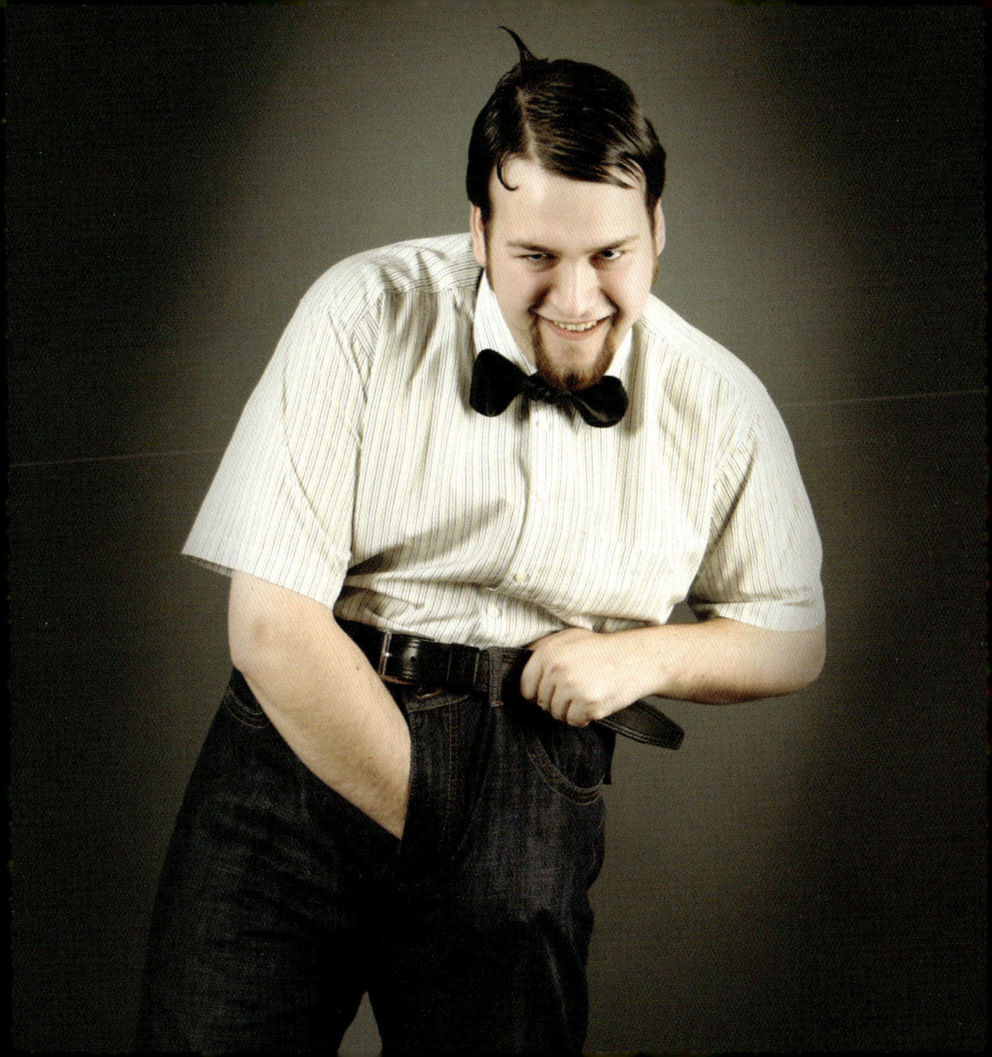

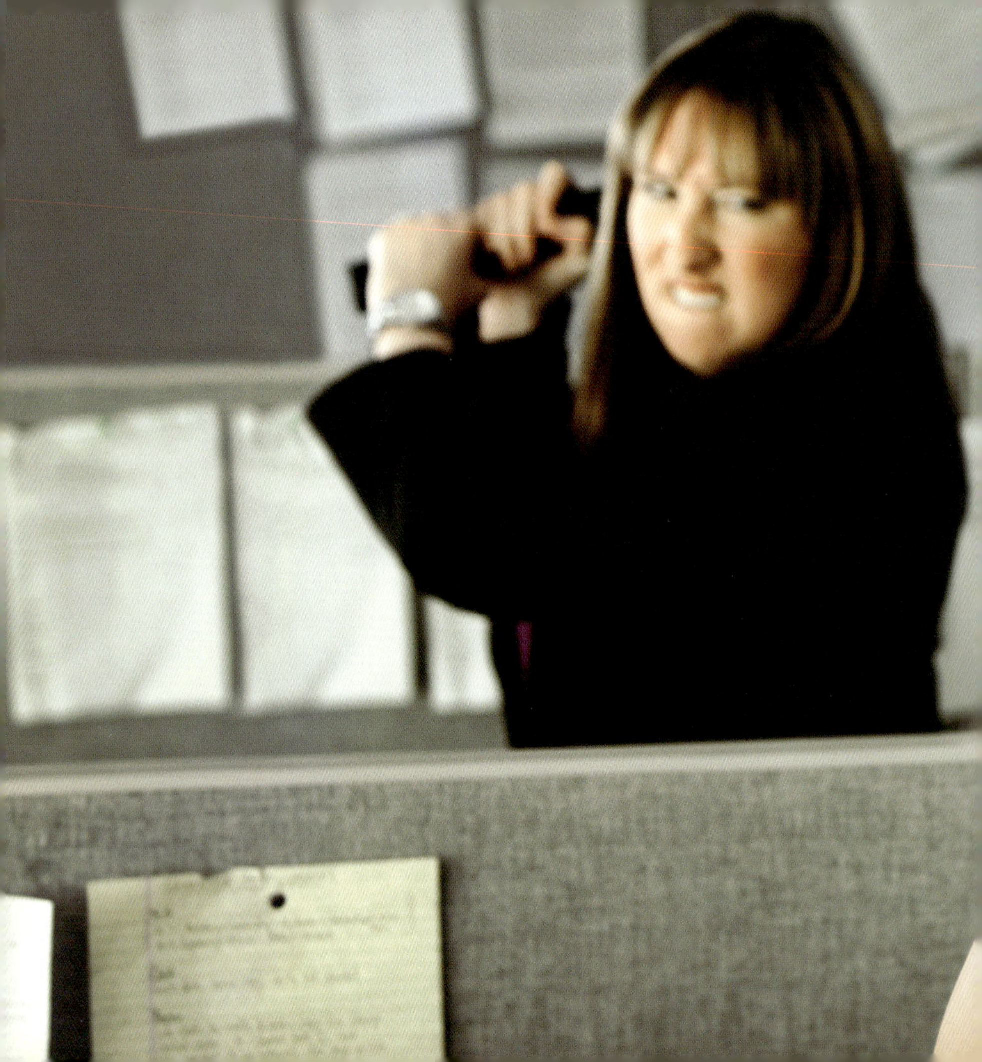

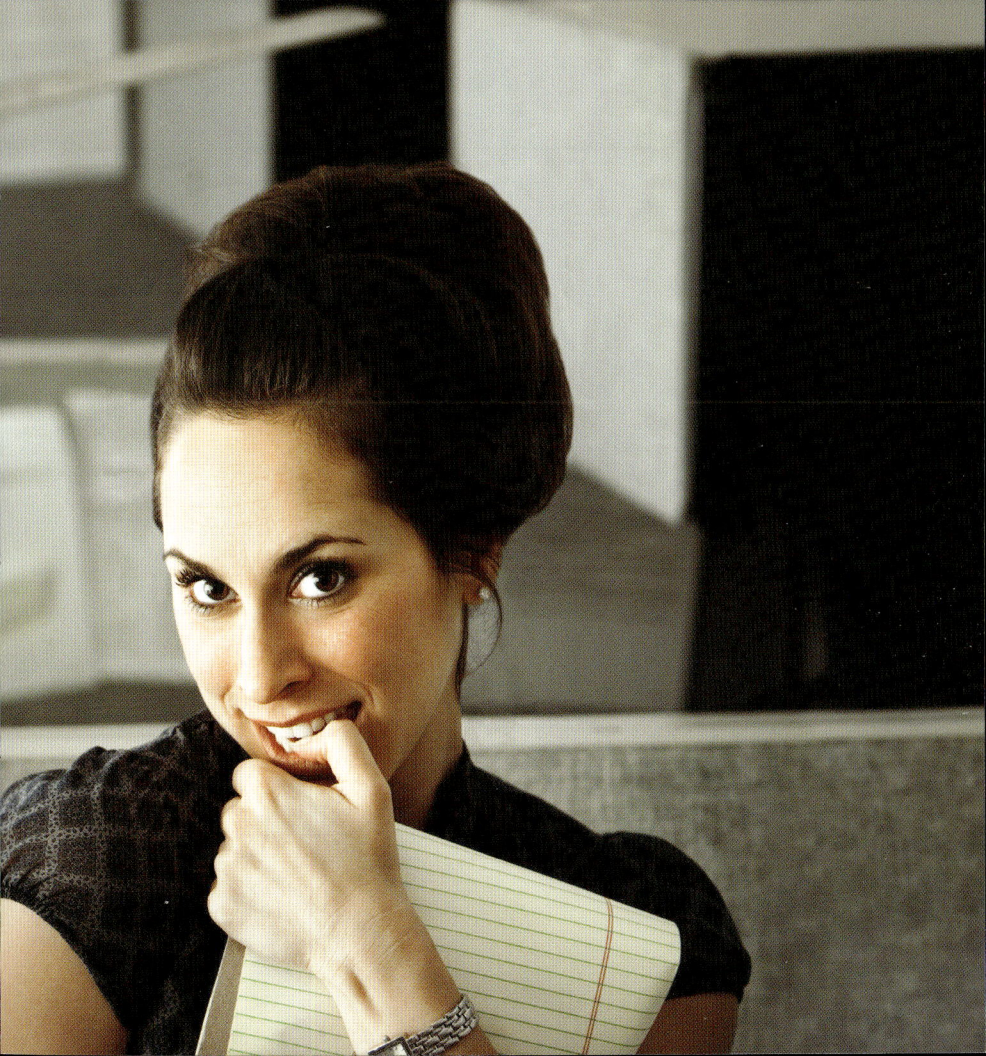

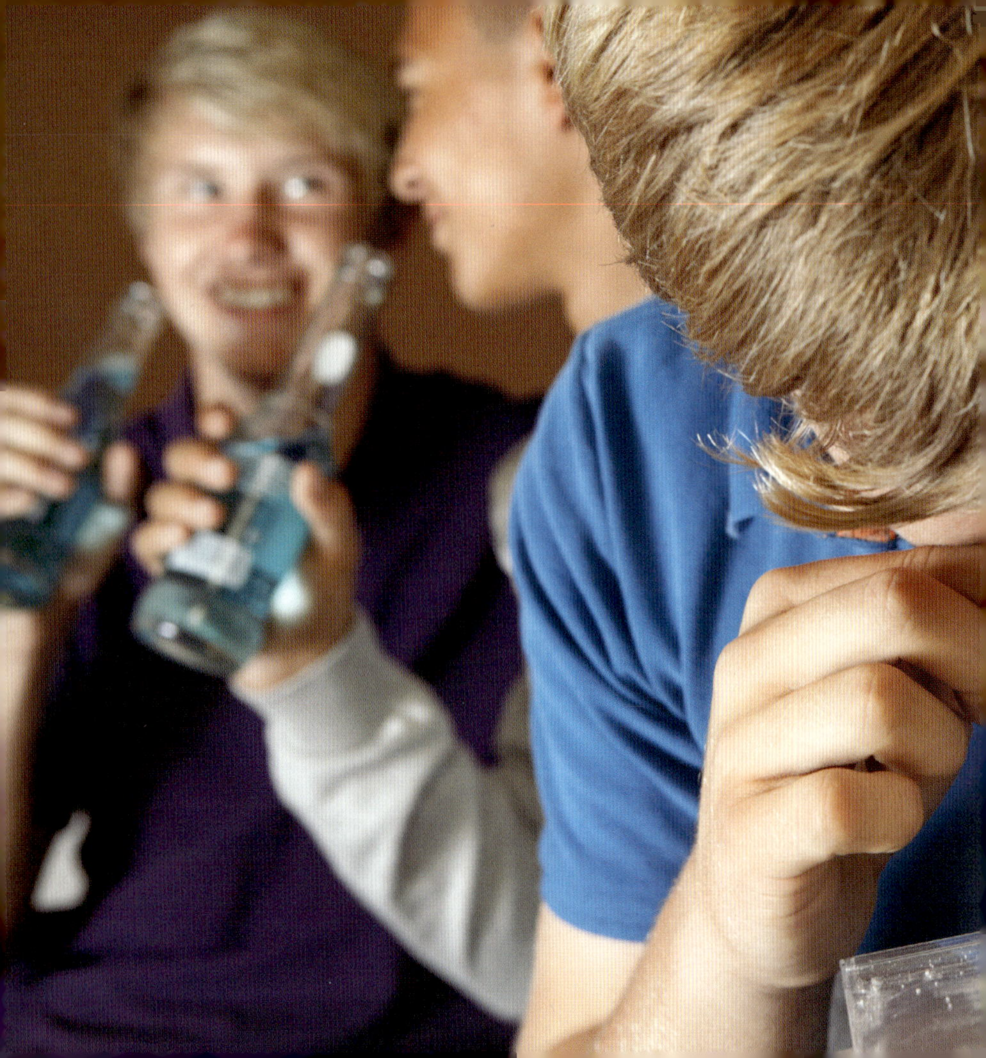

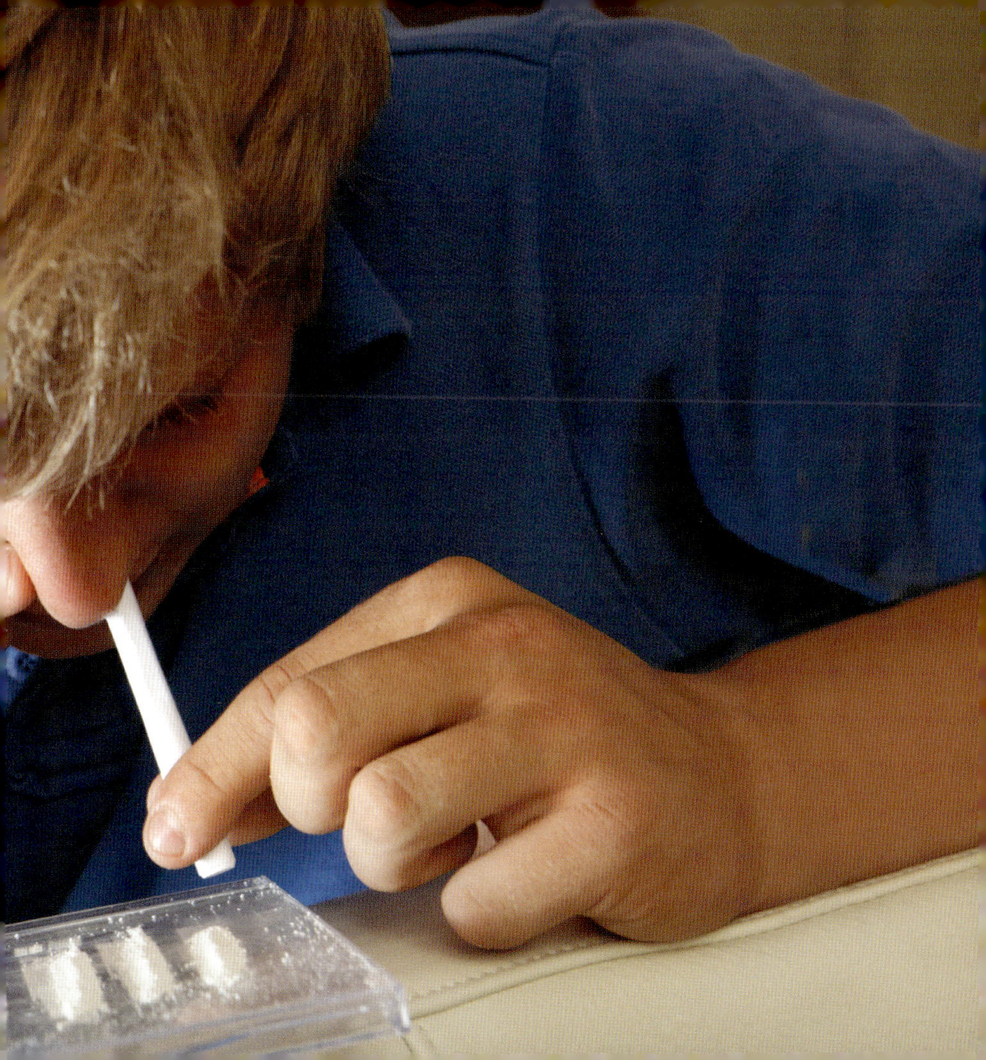

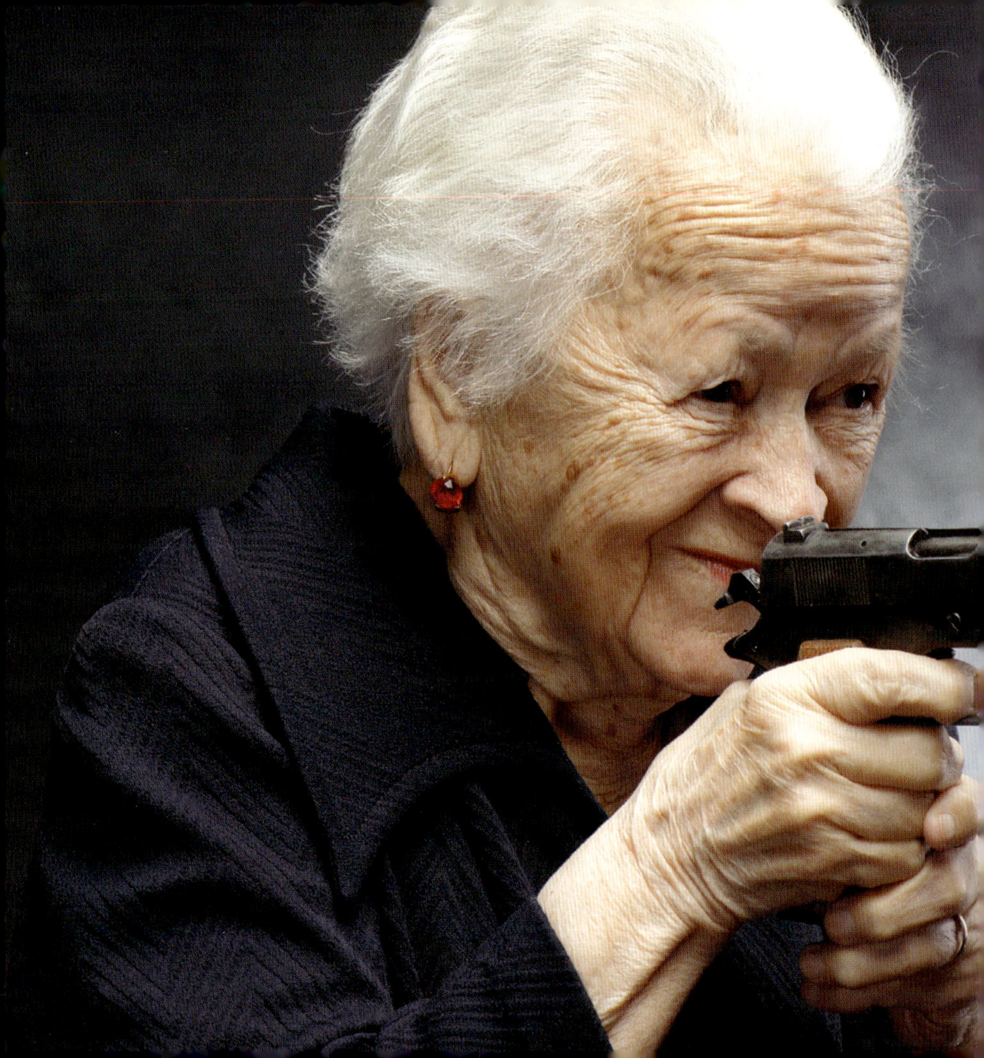

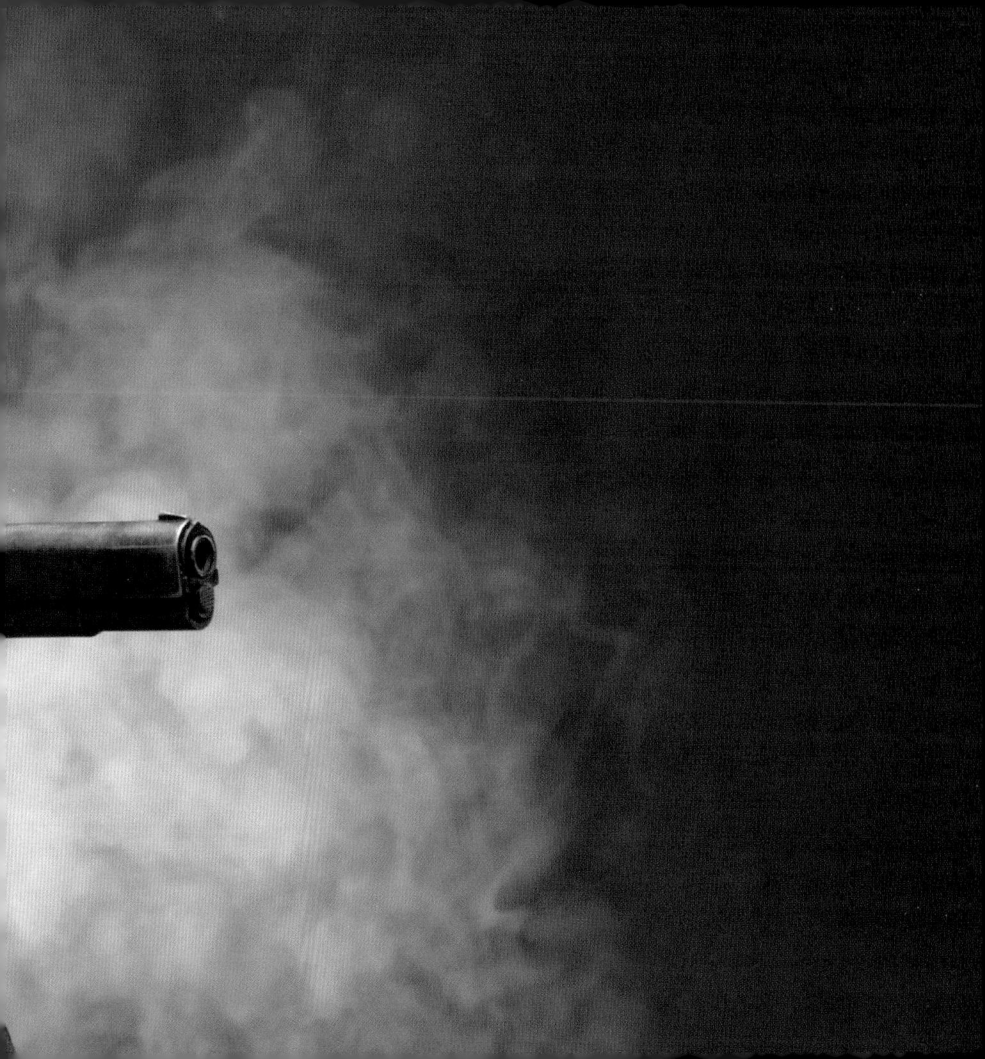

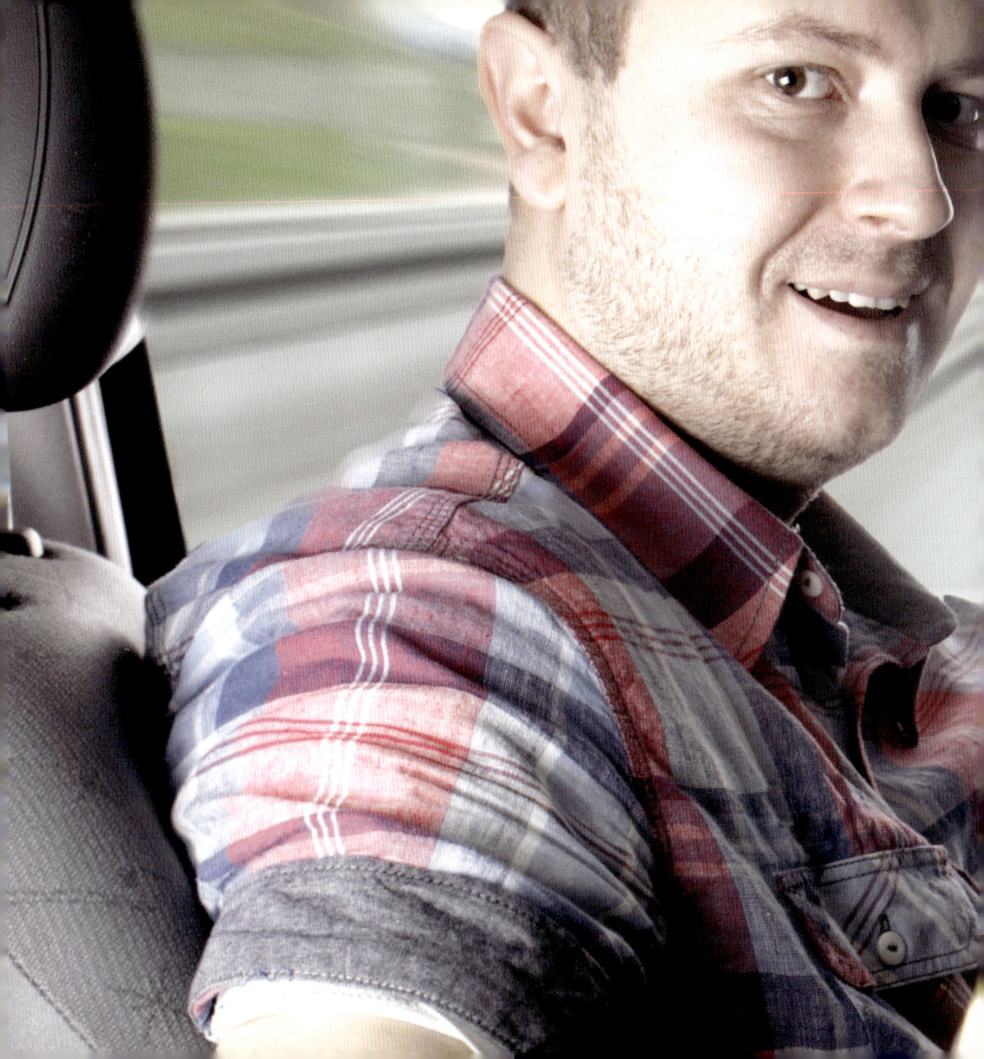

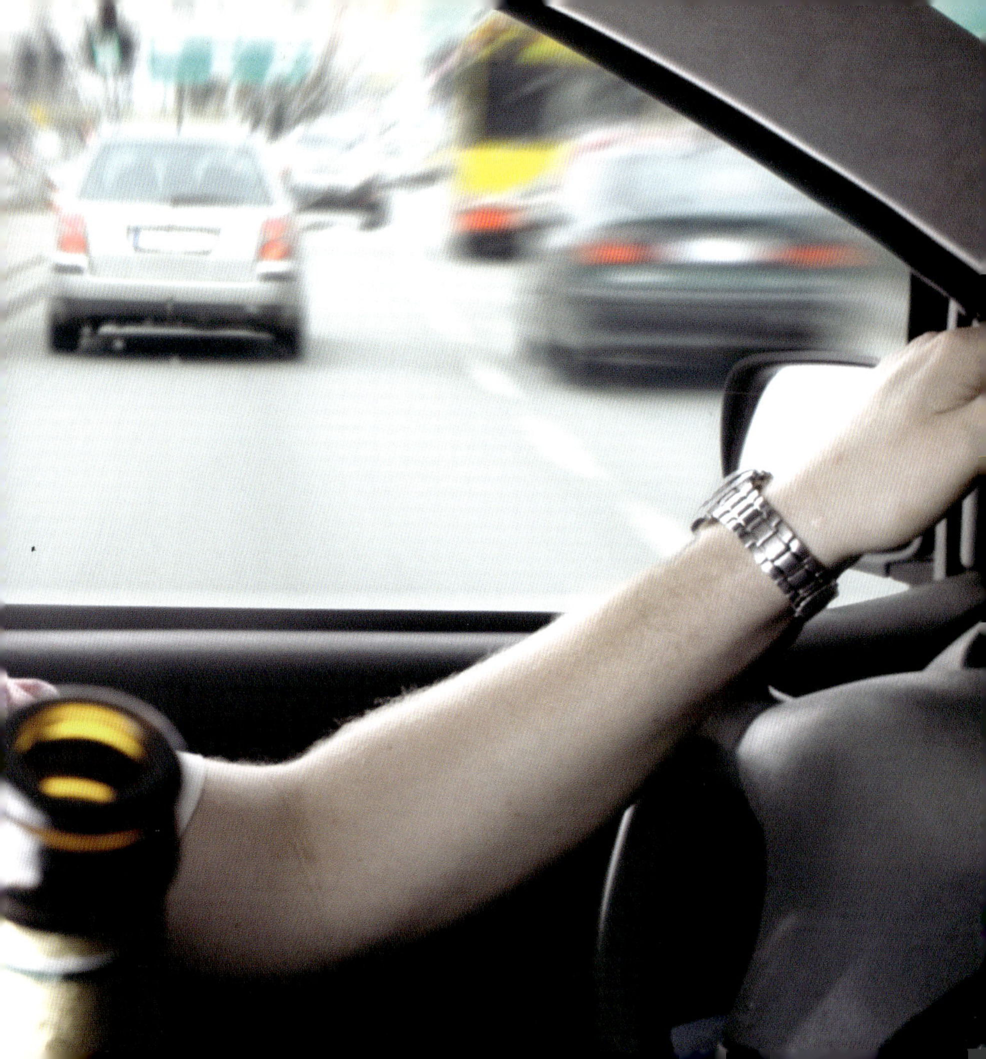

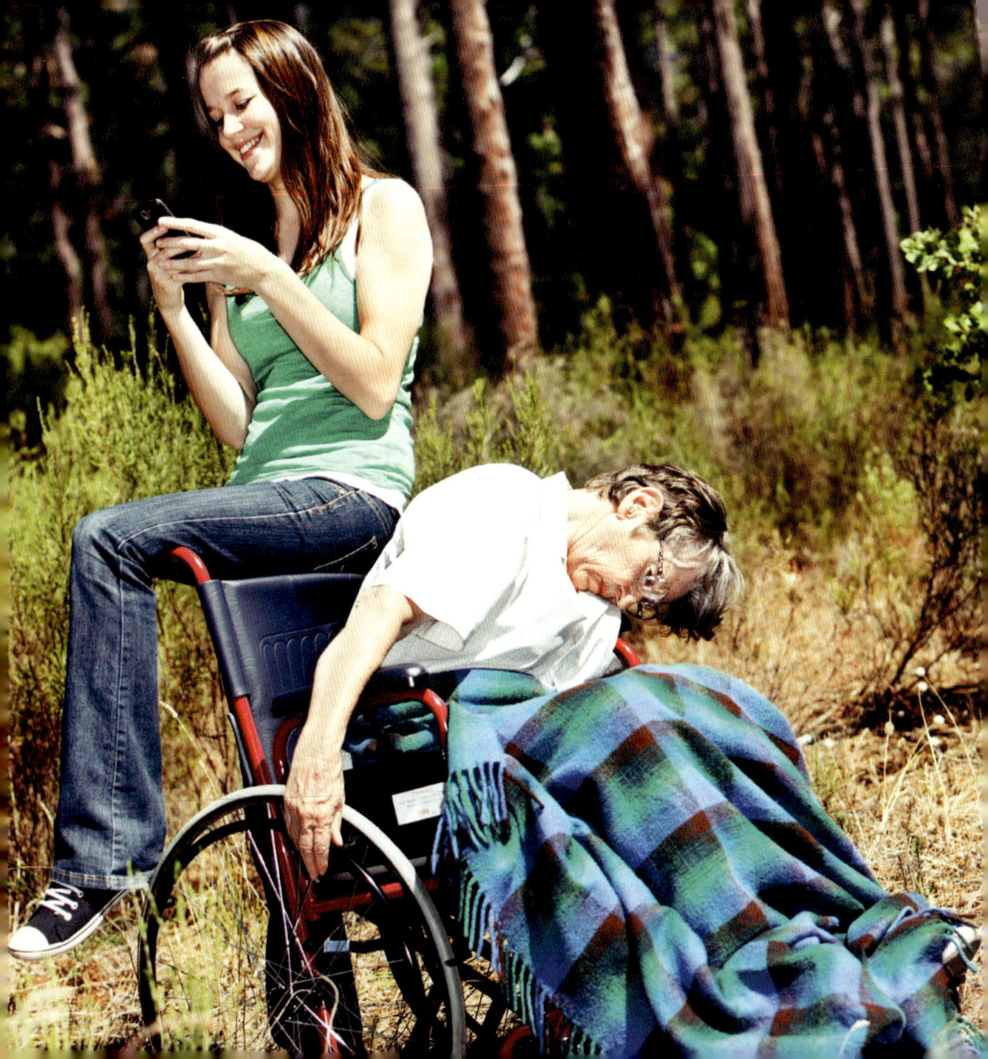

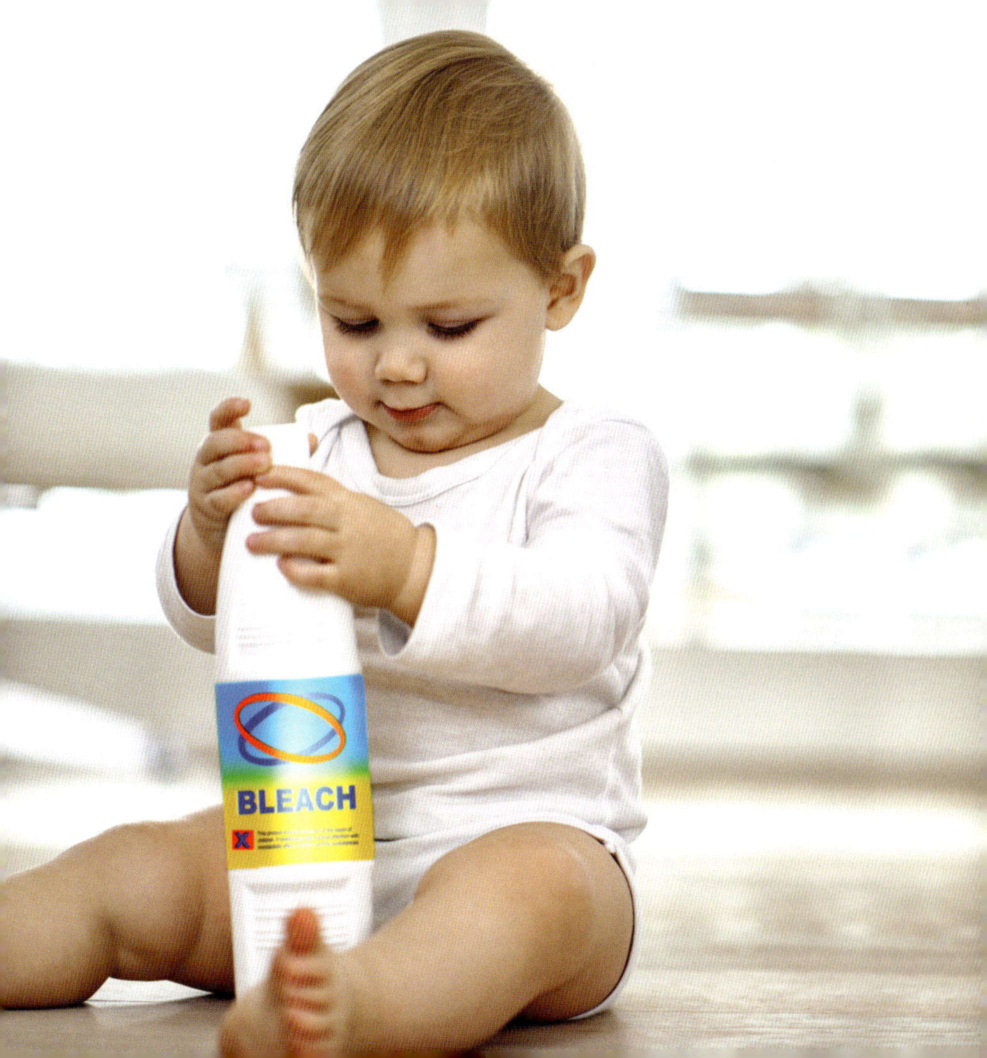
BLEACH

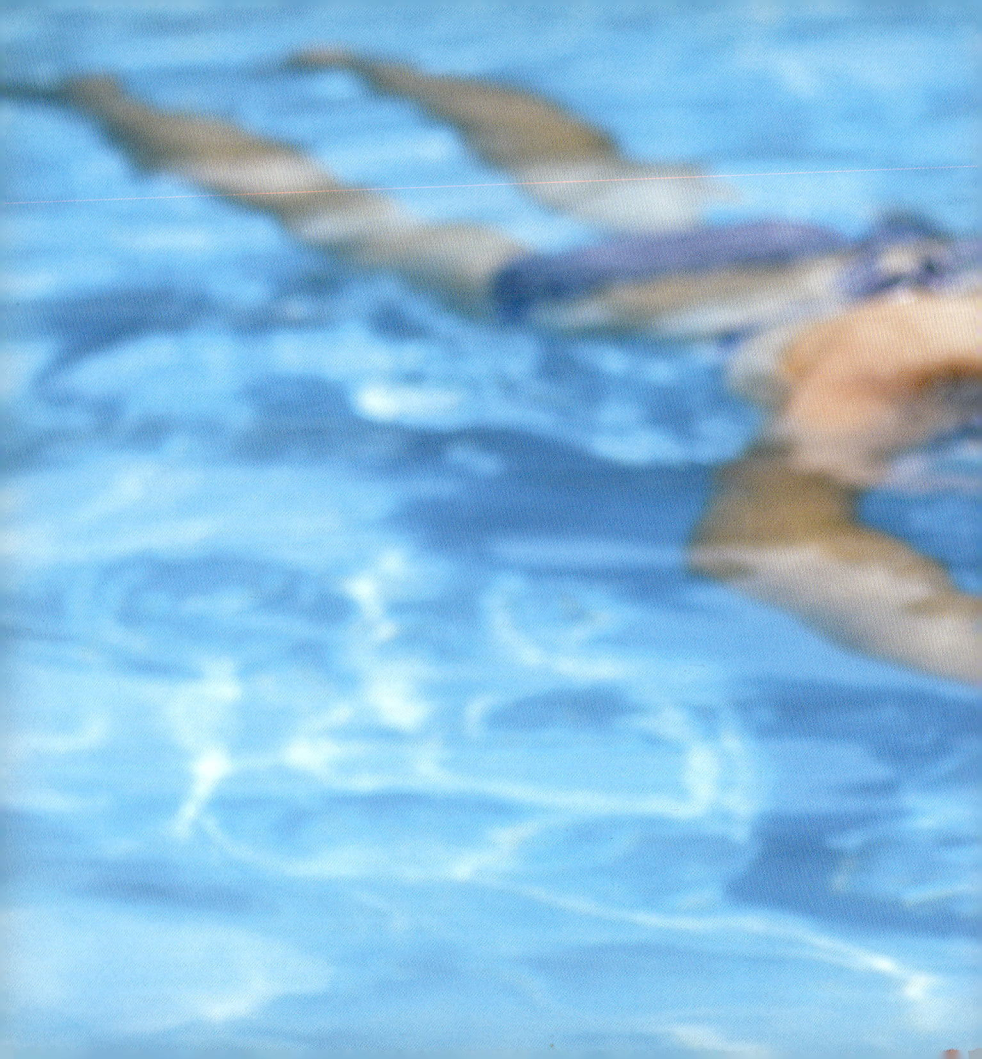

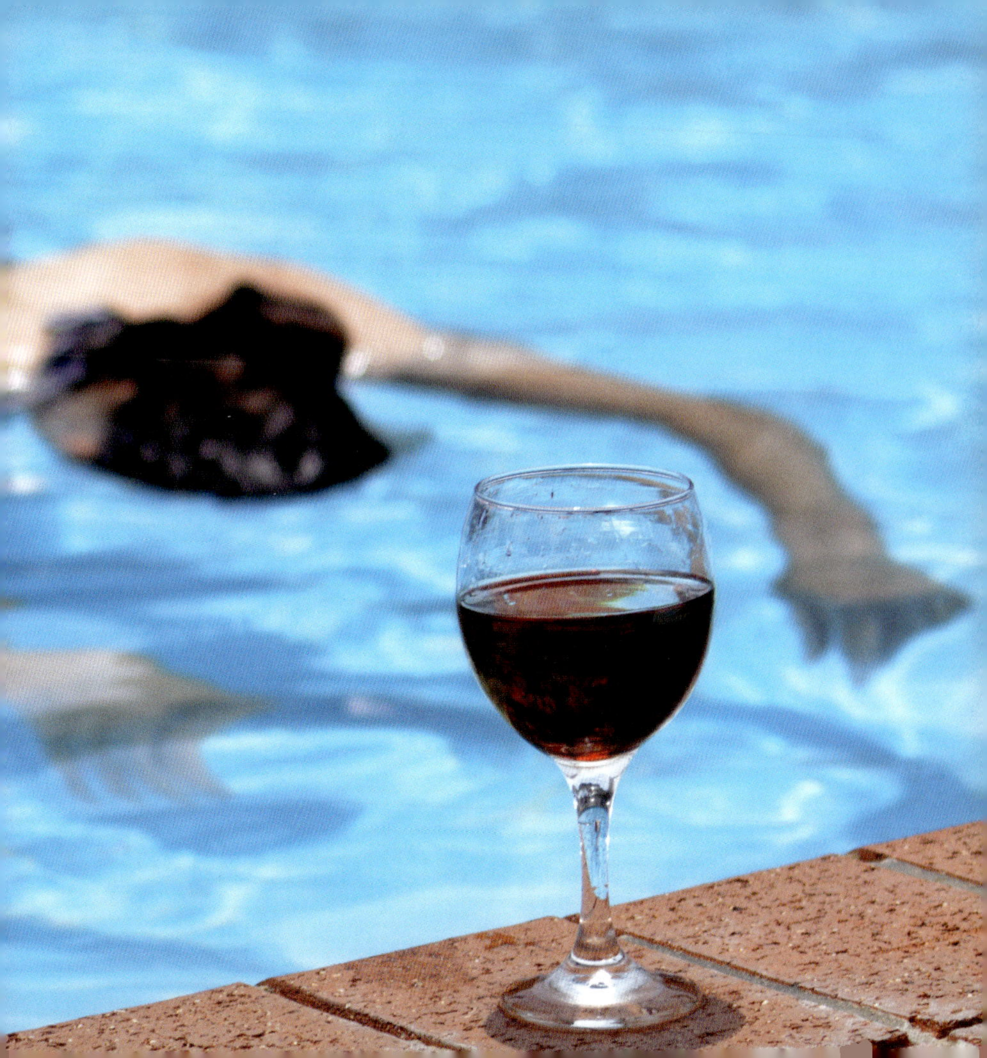

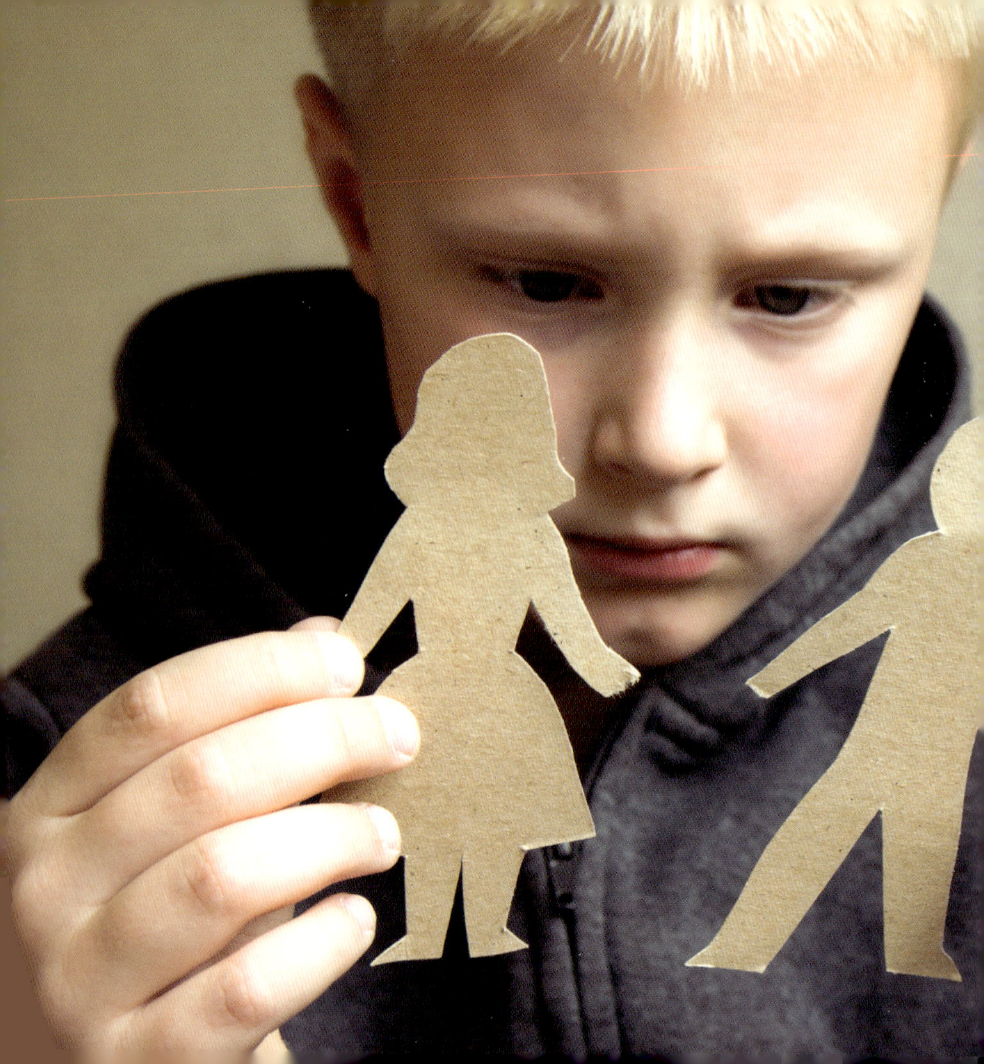

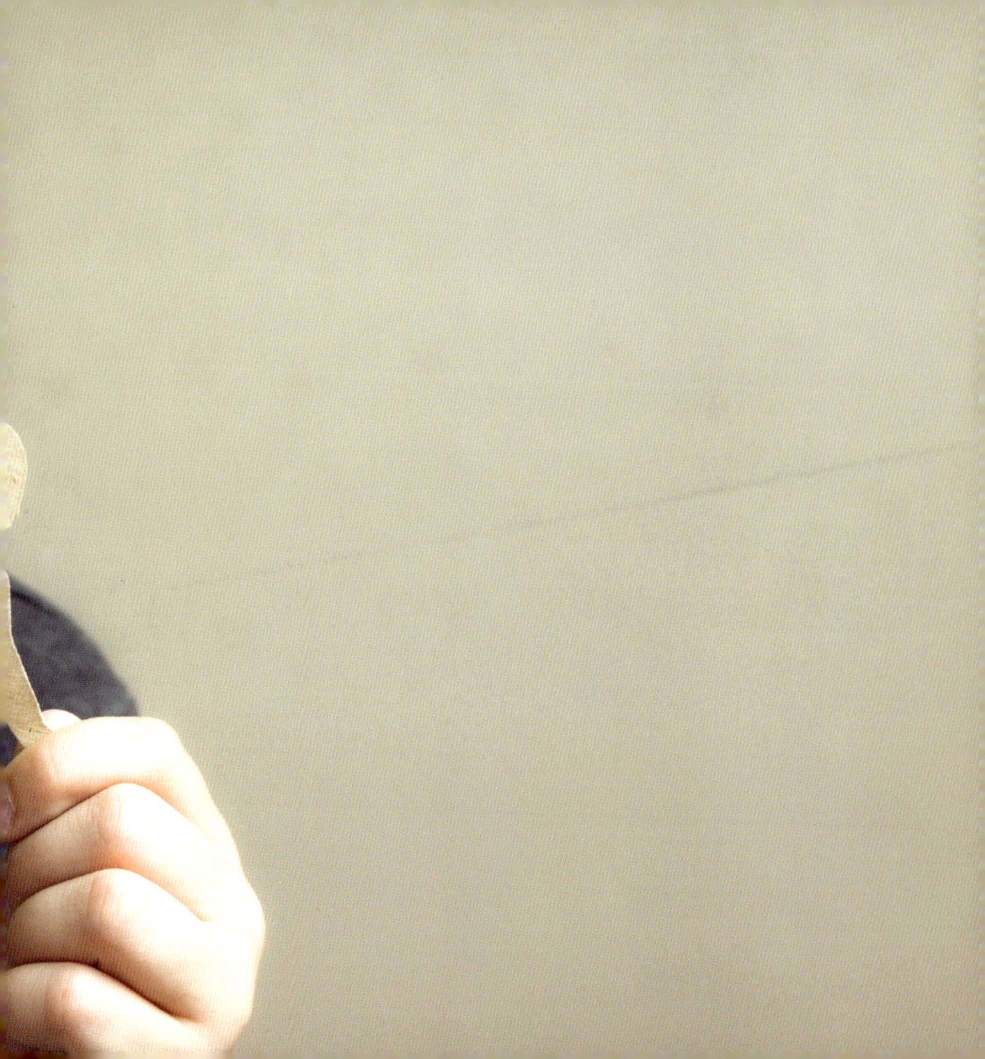

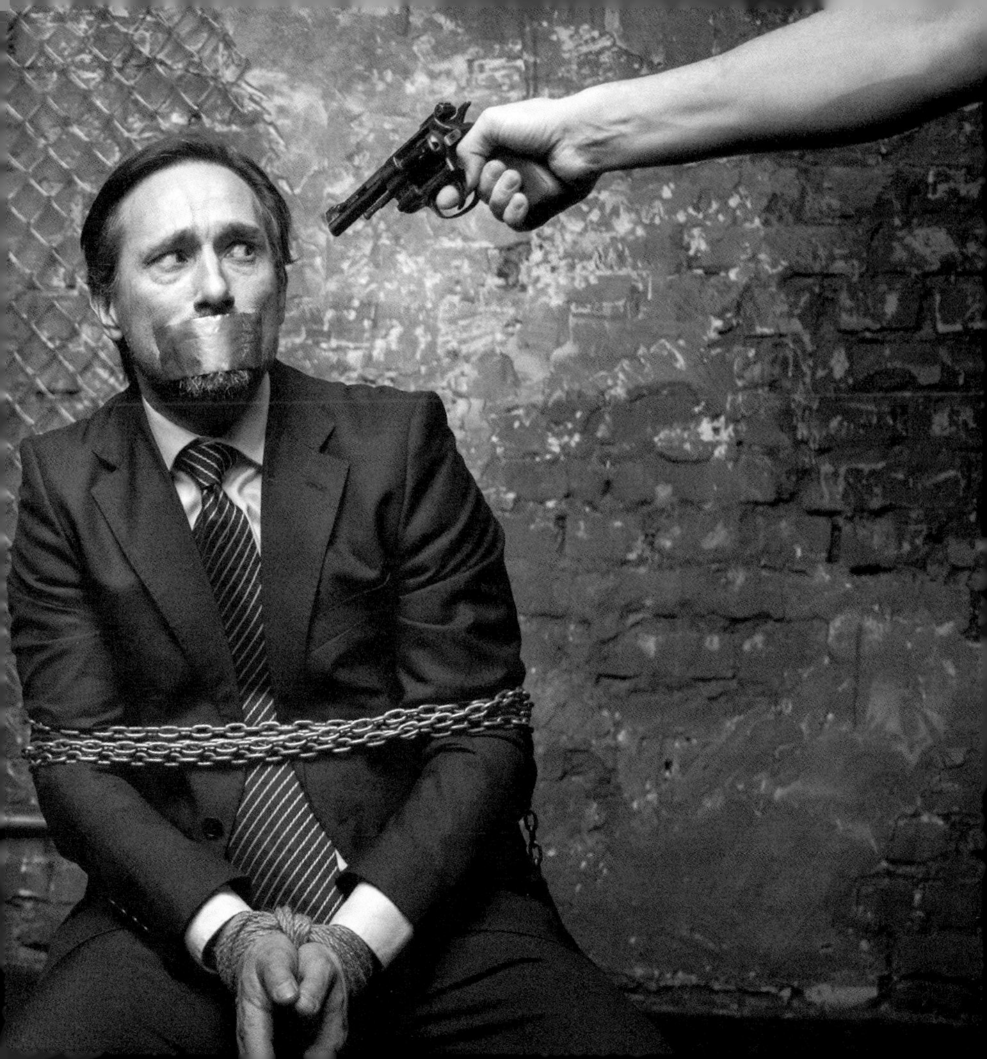

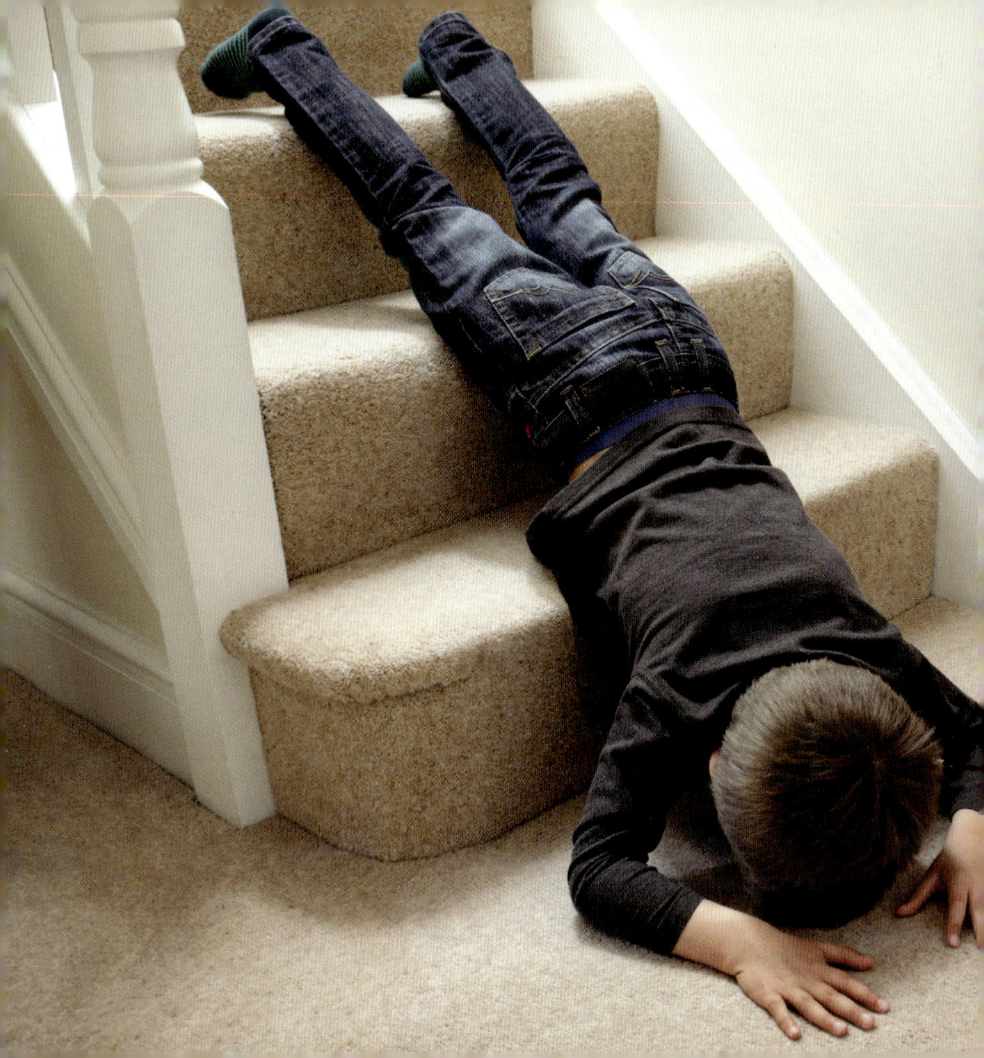

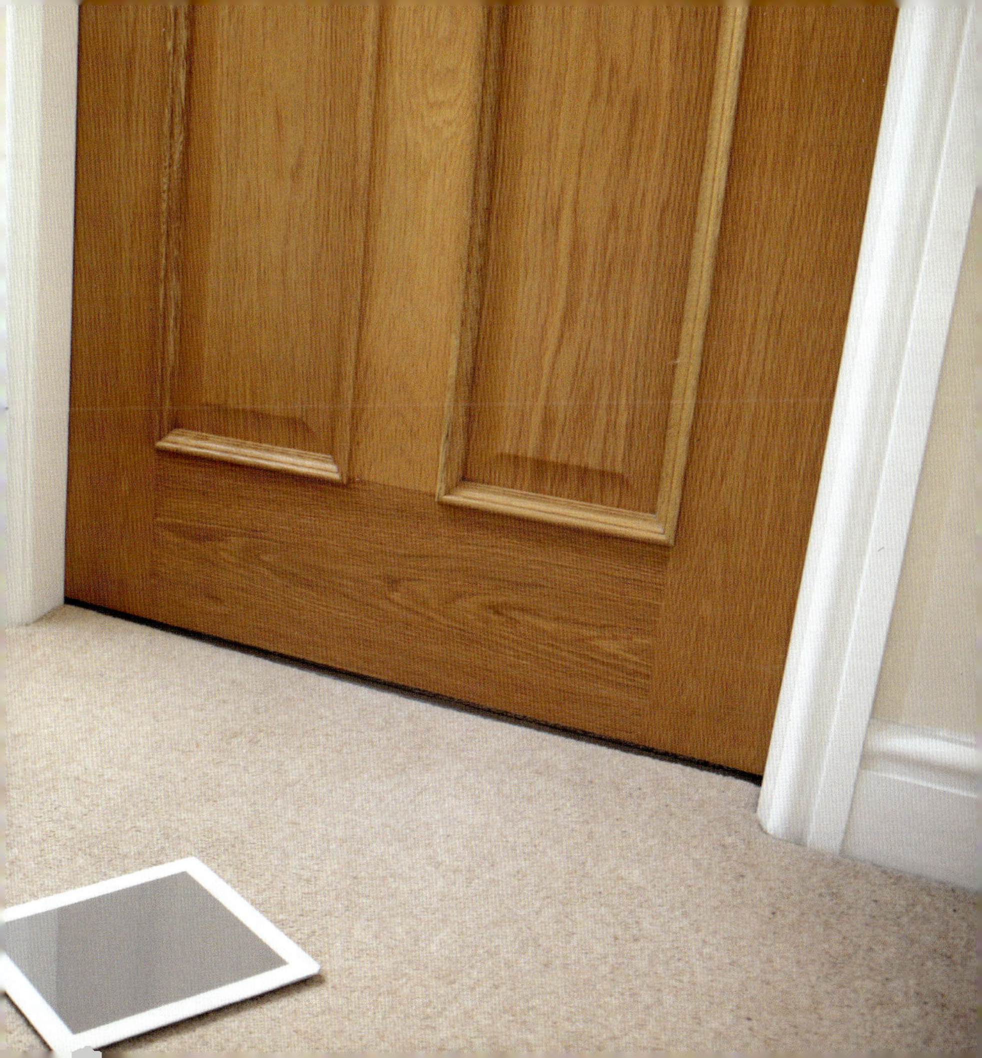

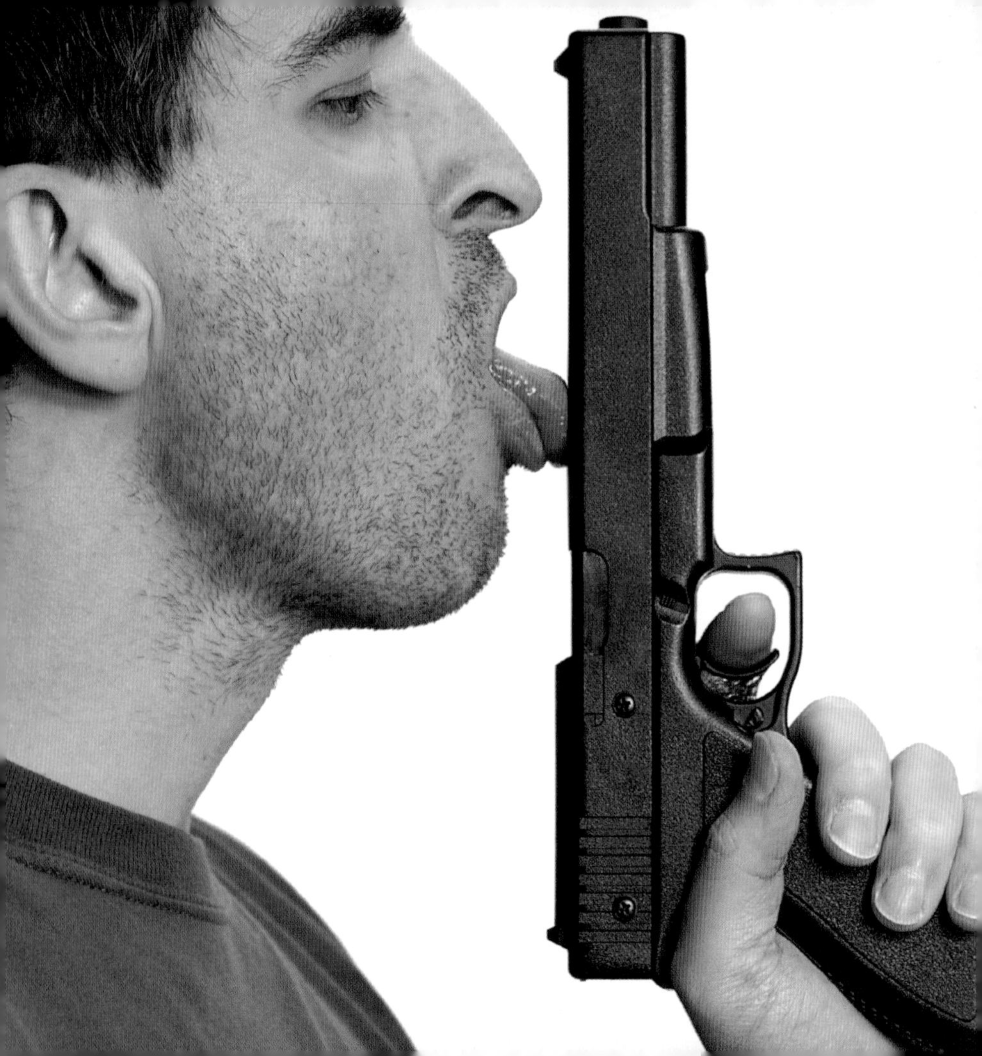

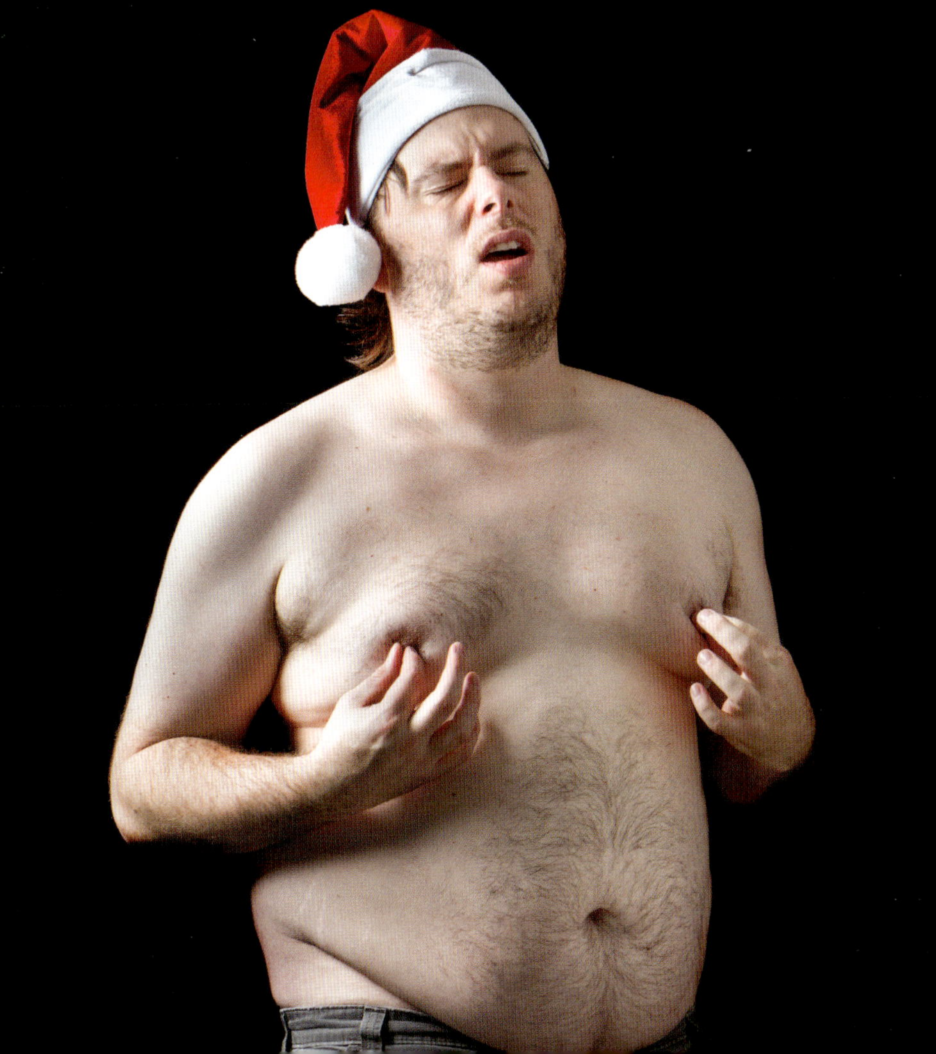

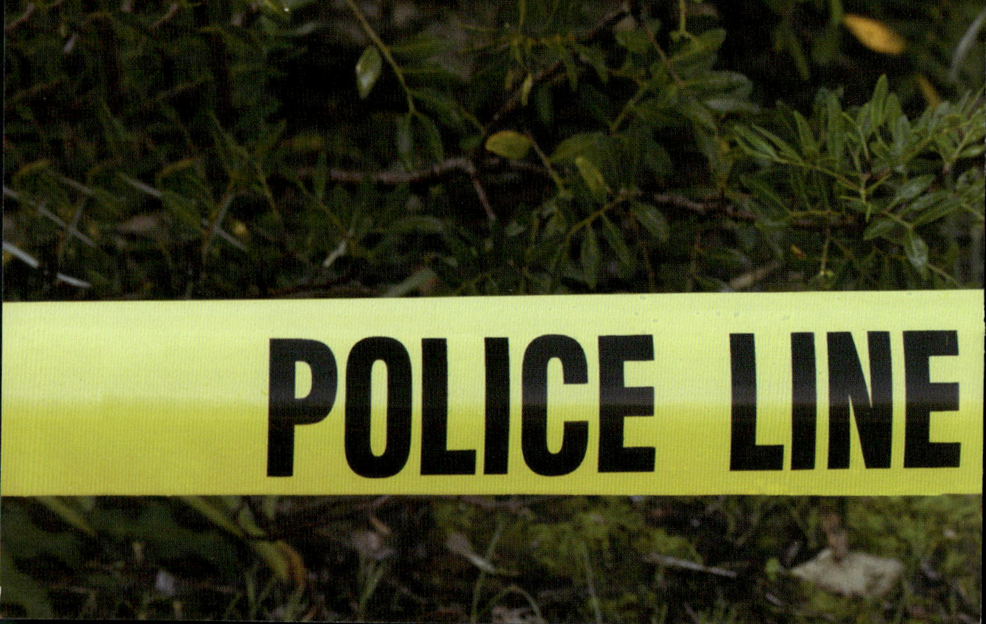
POLICE LINE

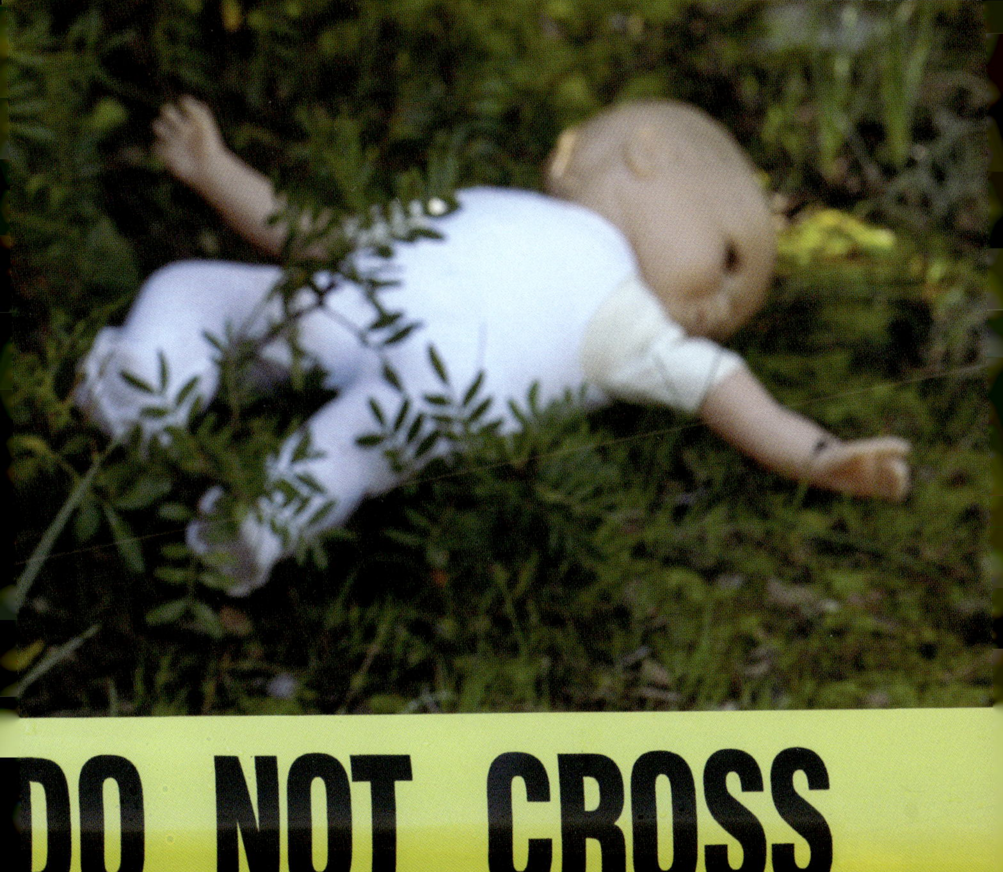
DO NOT CROSS

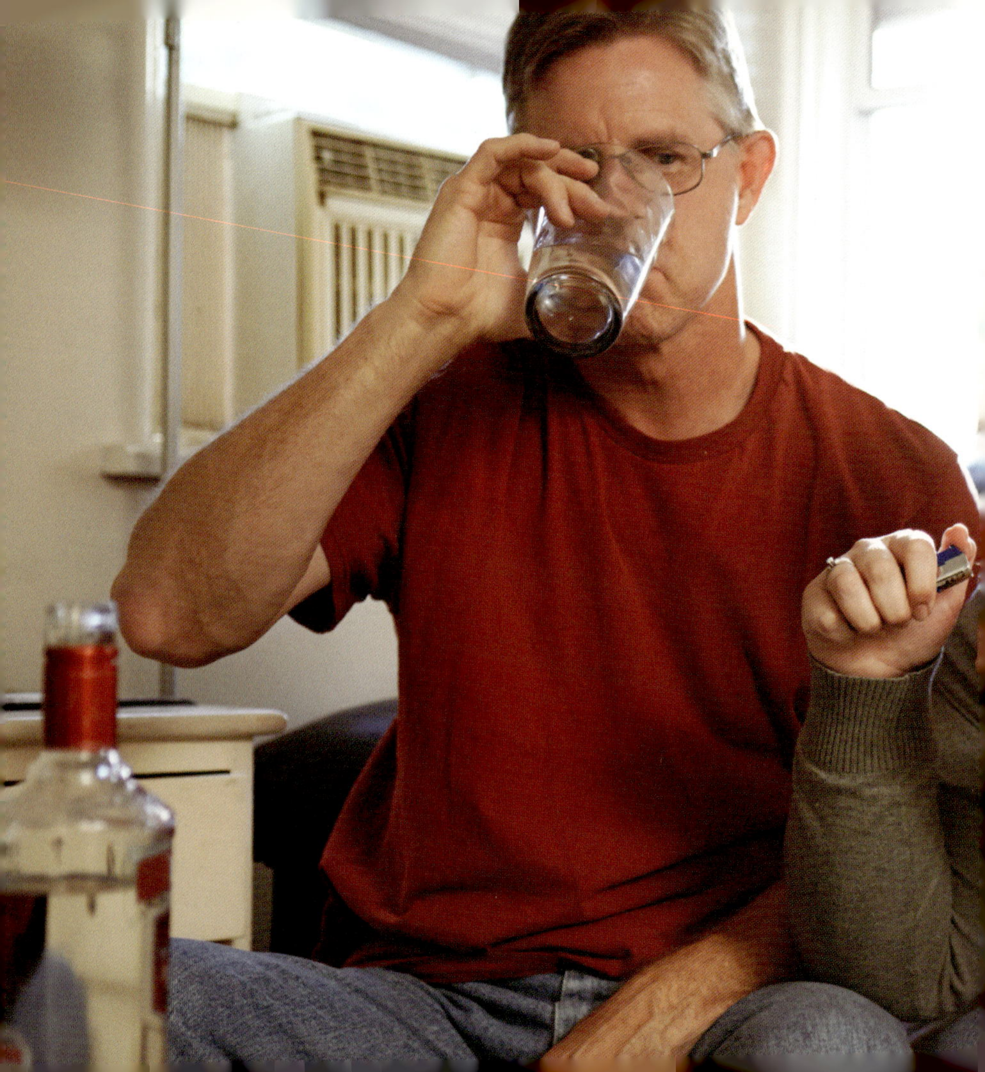

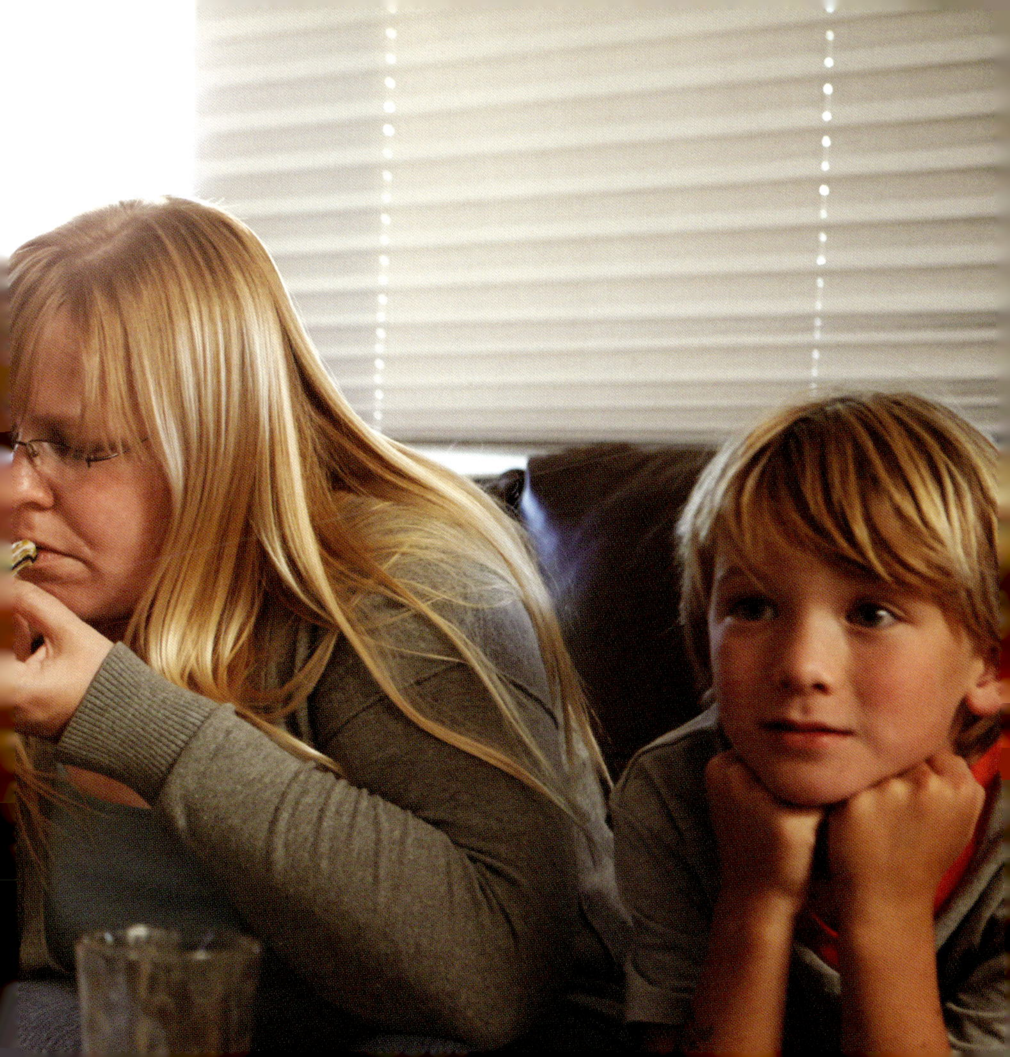

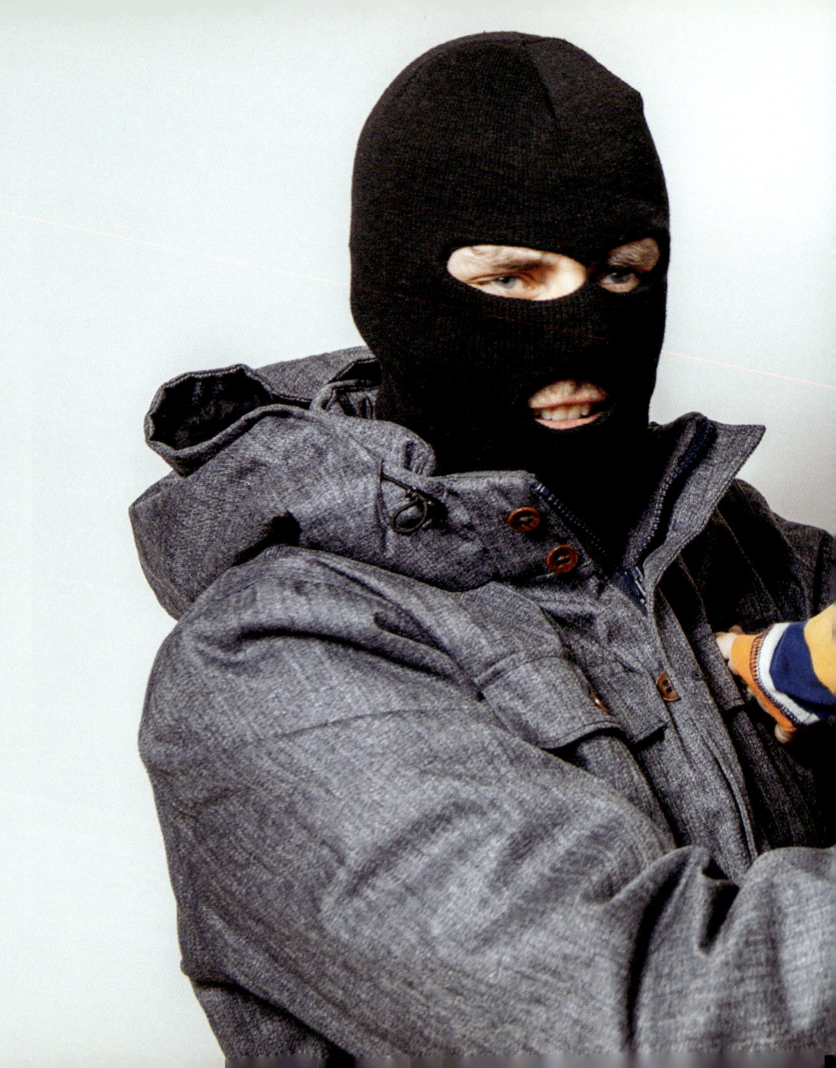

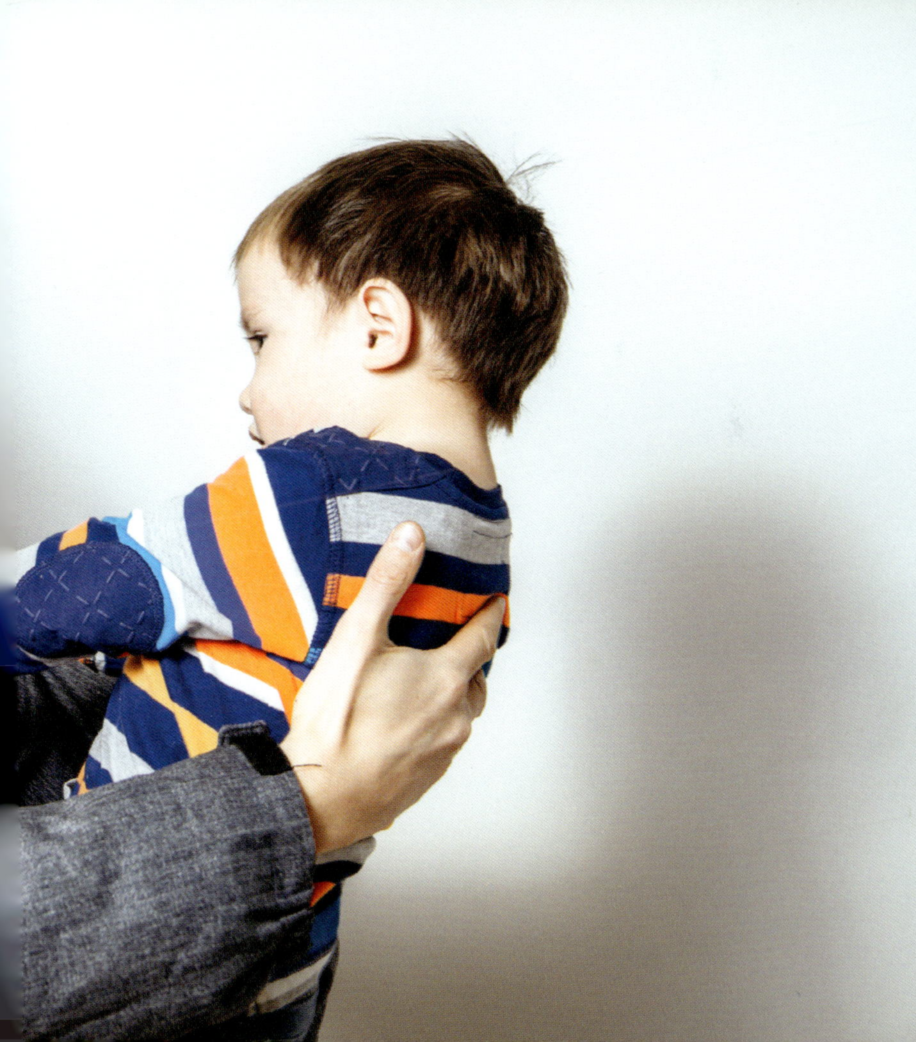

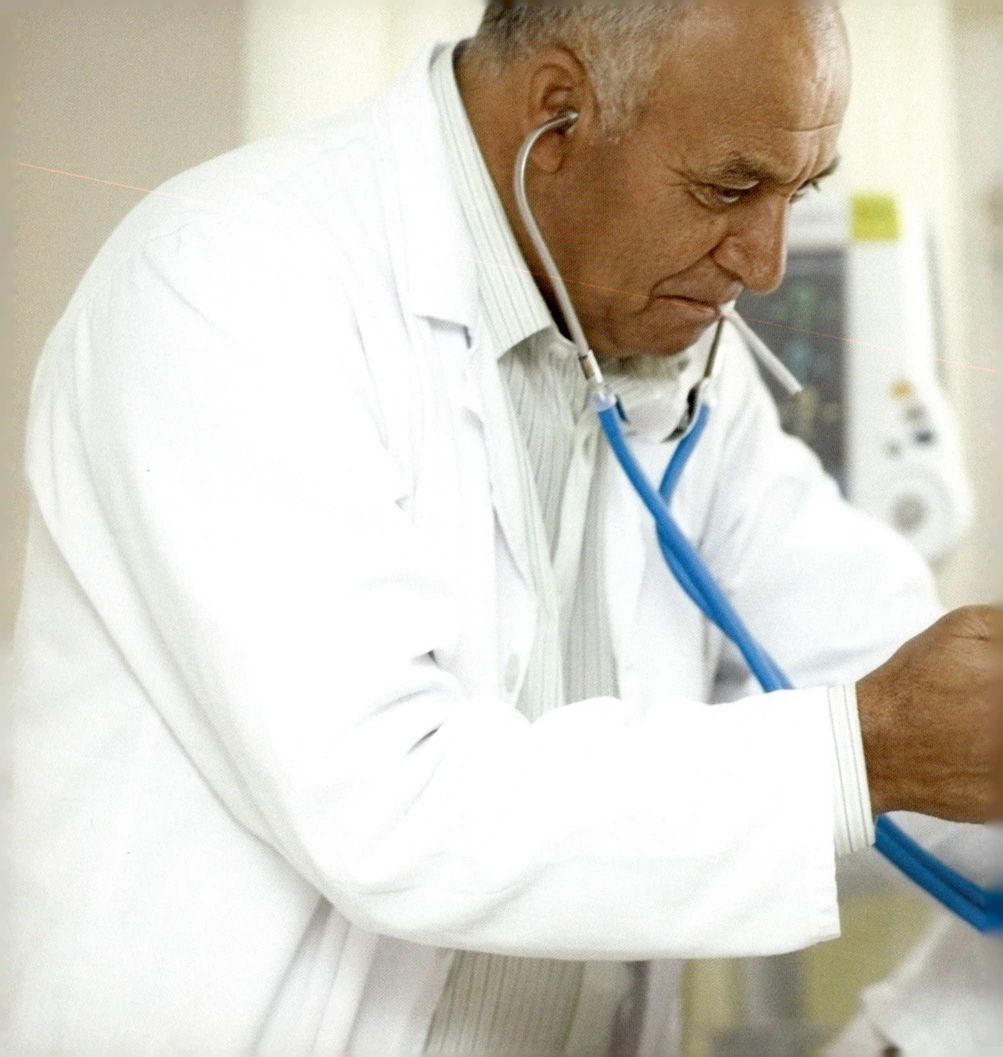

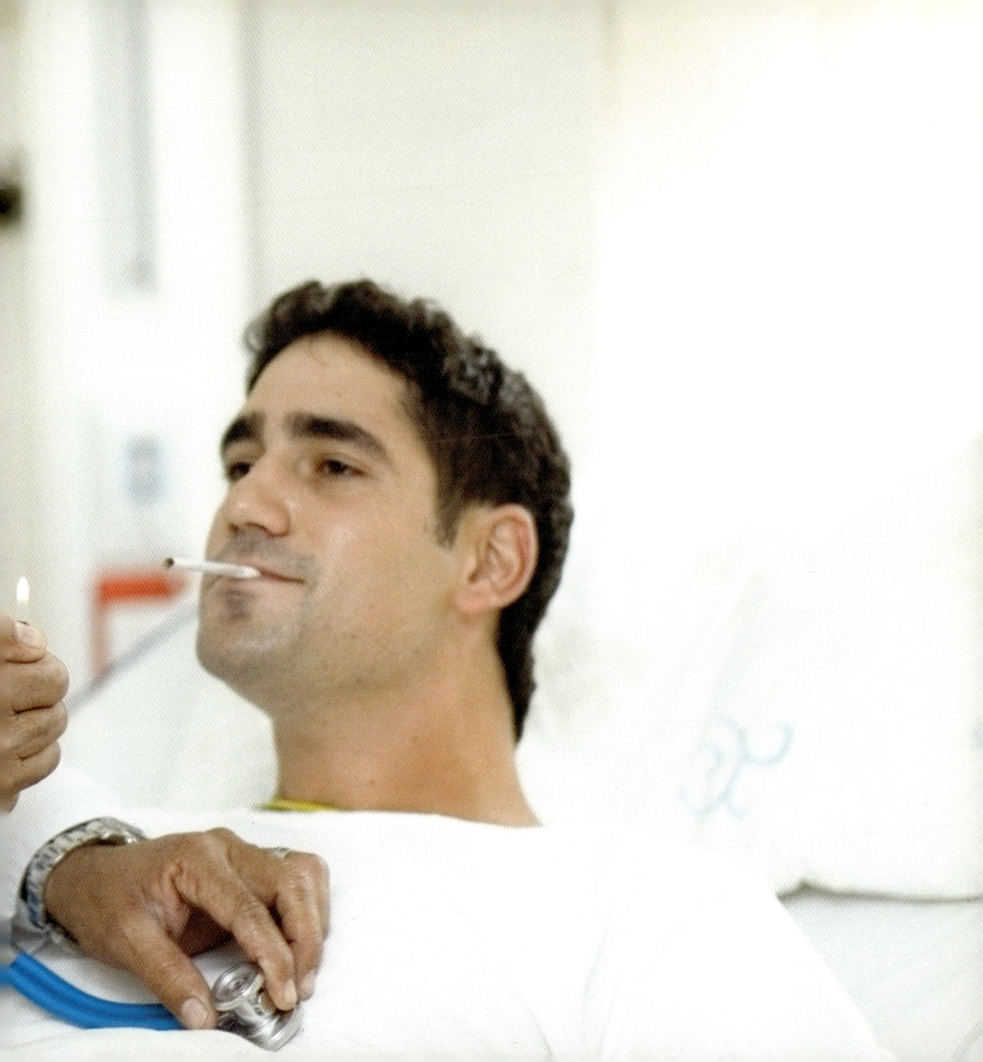

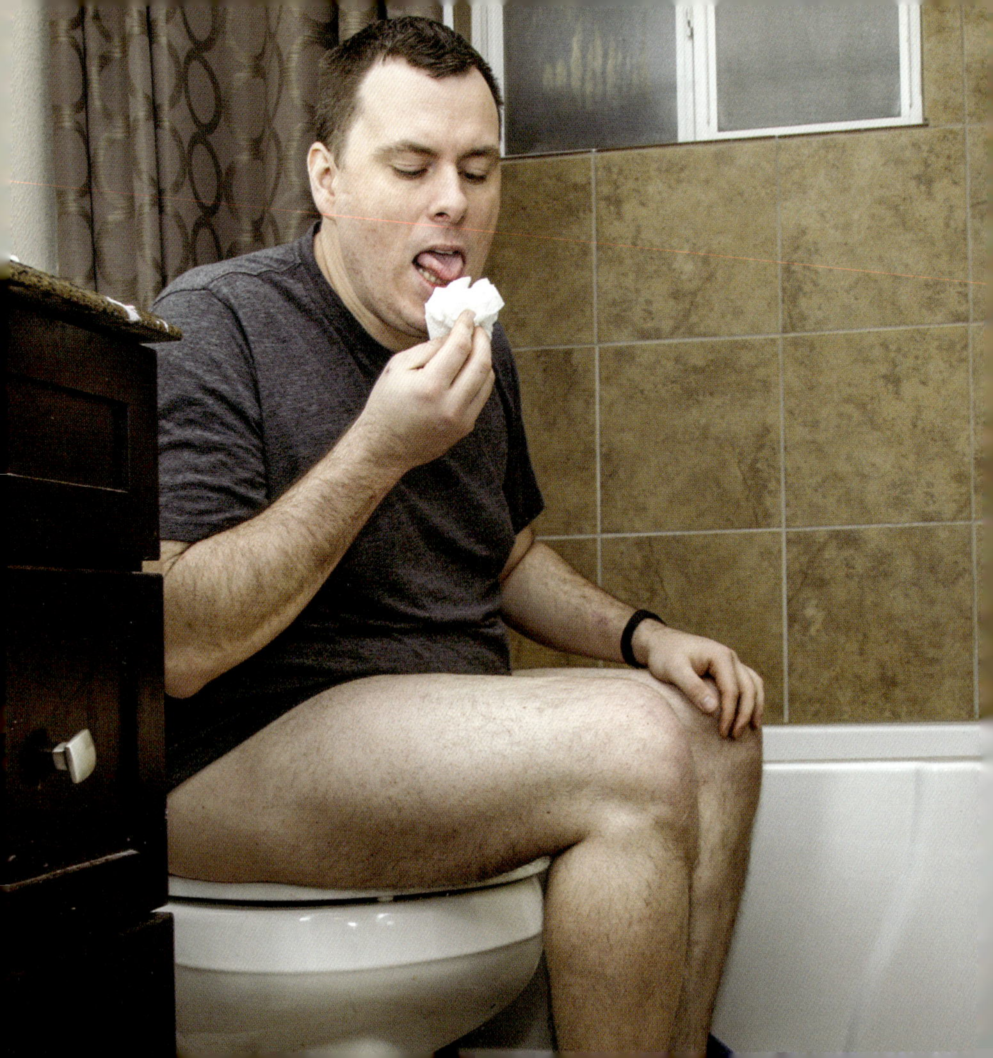

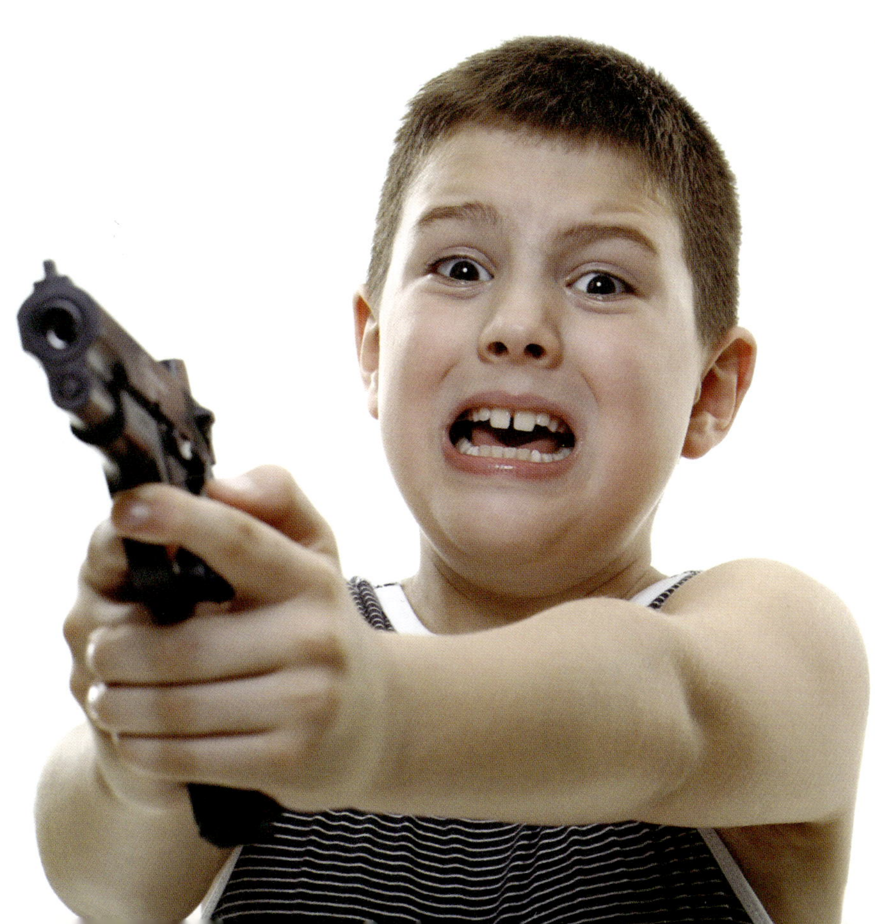

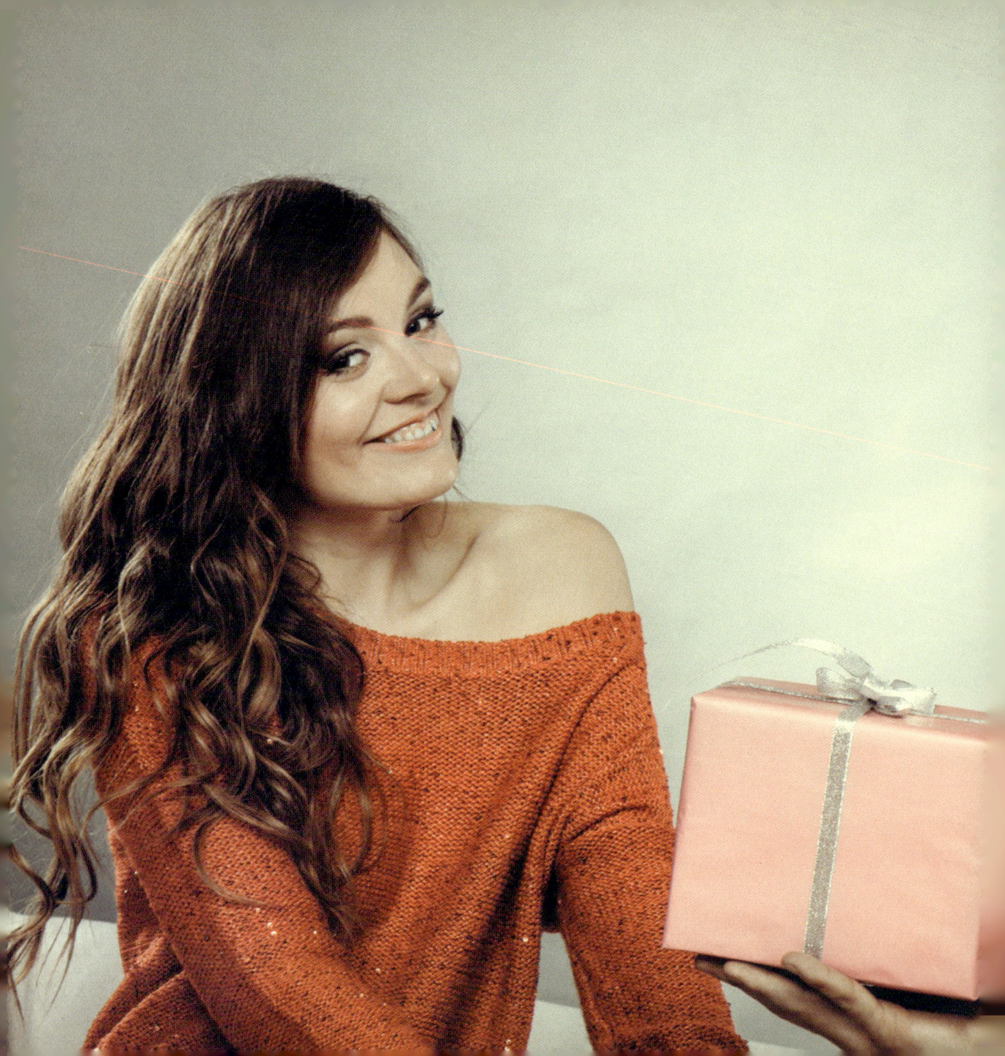

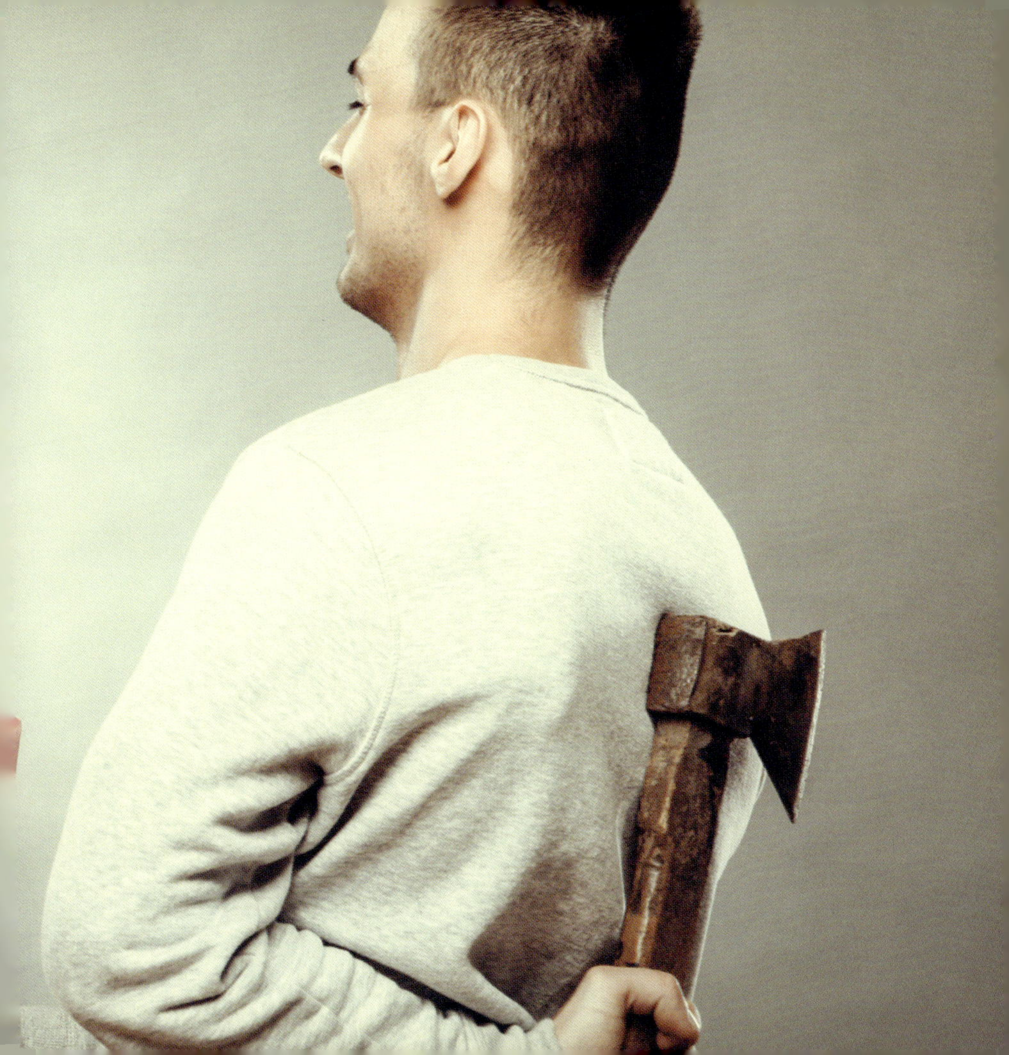

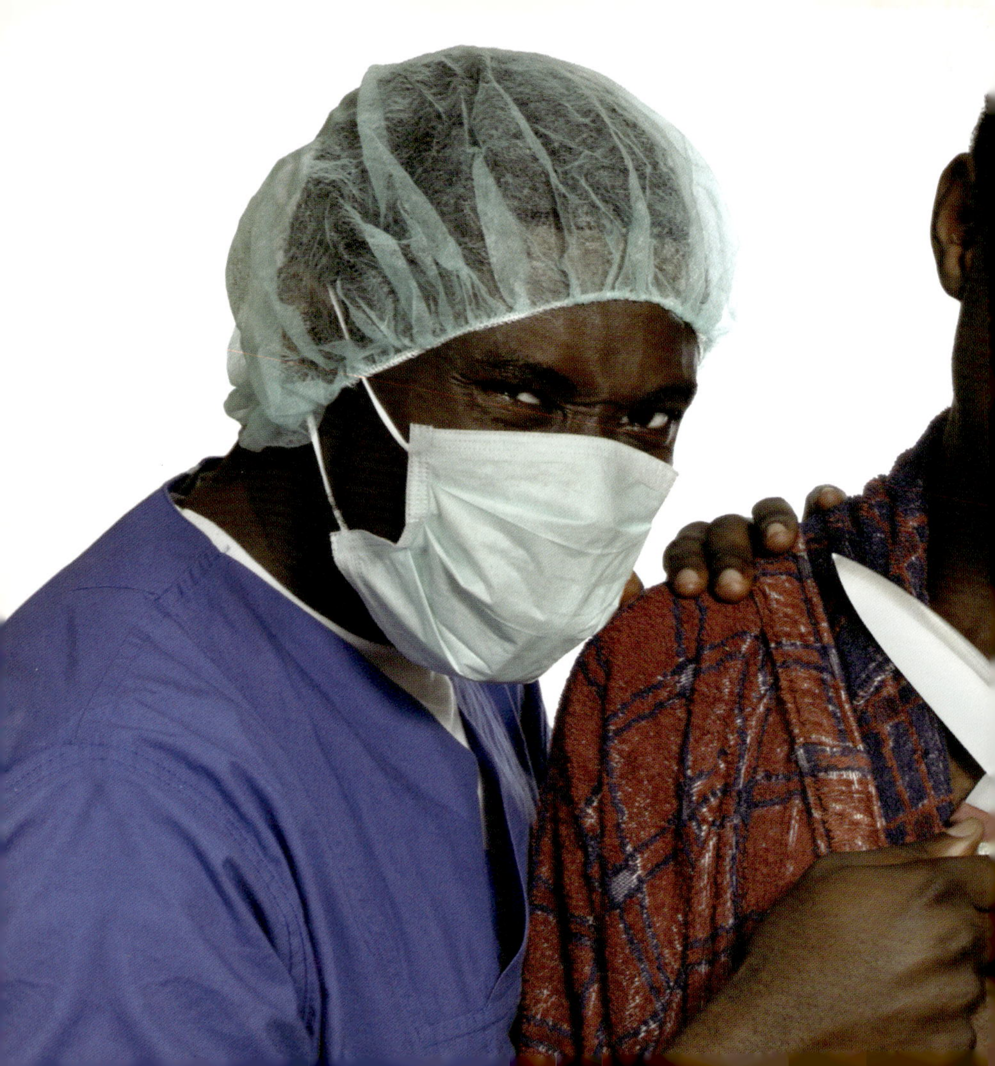

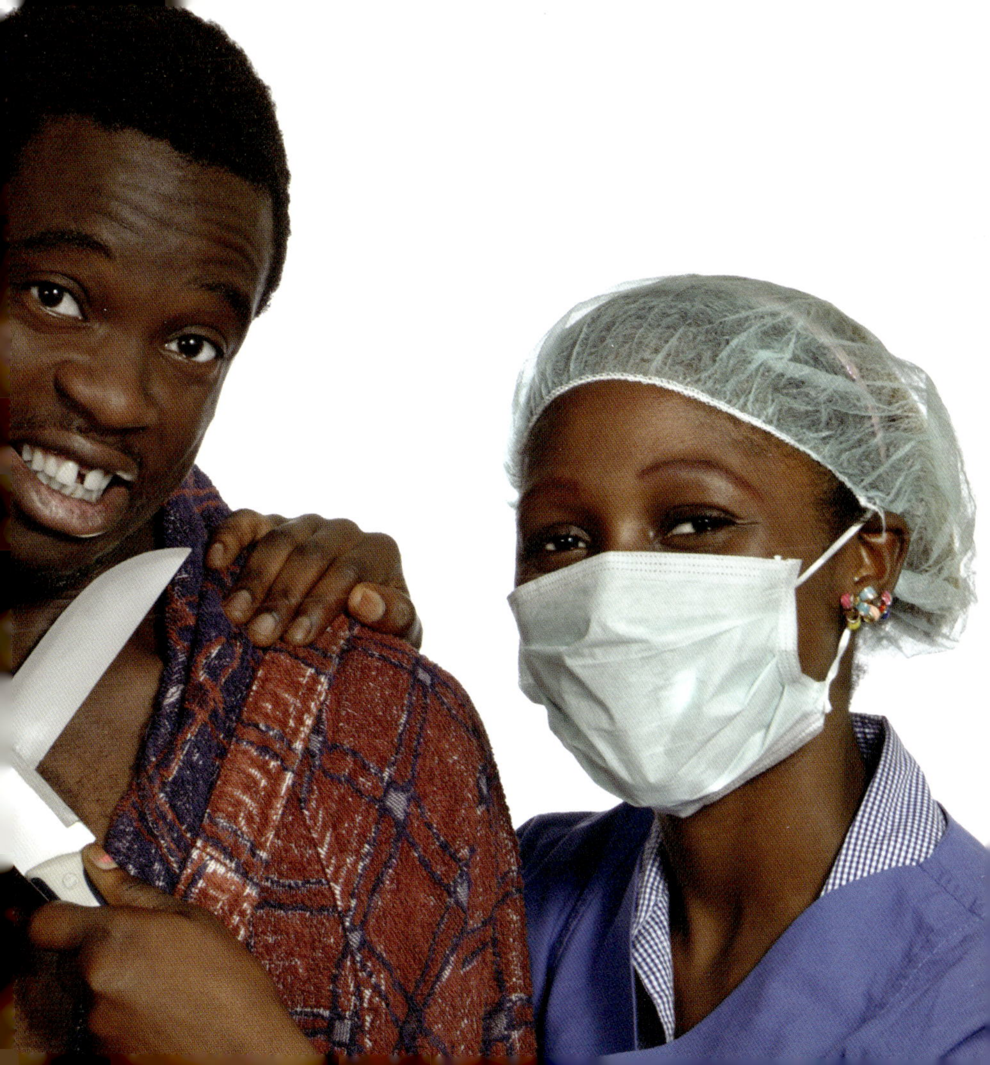

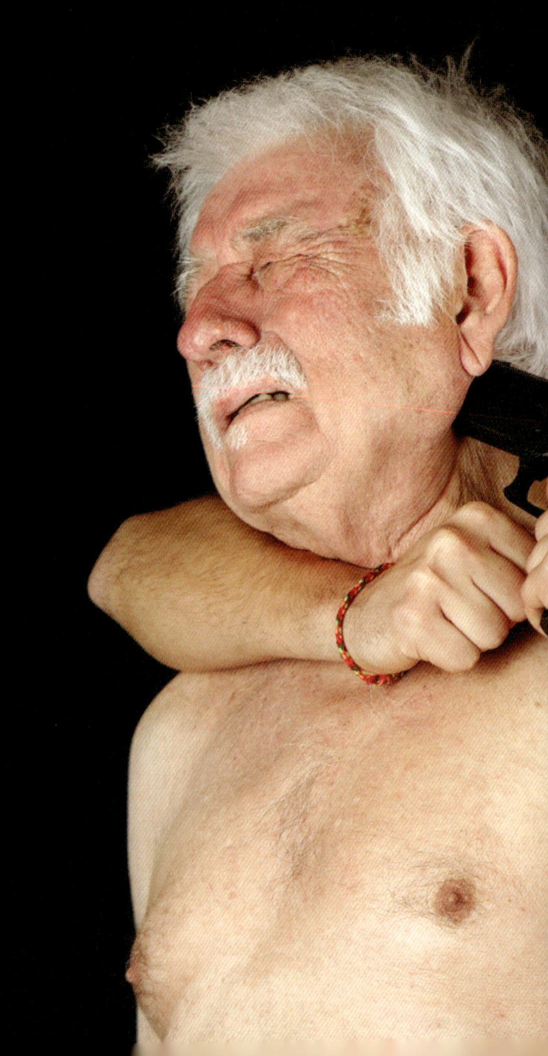

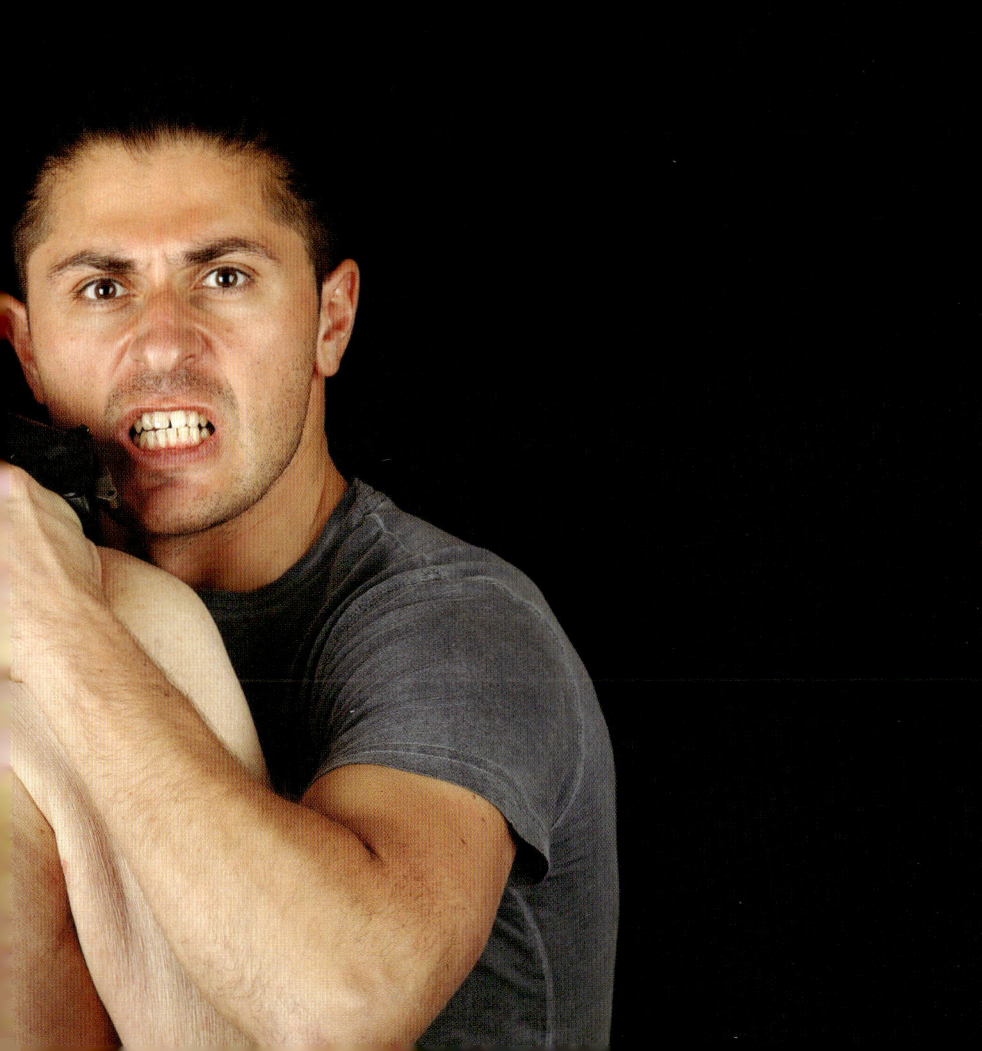

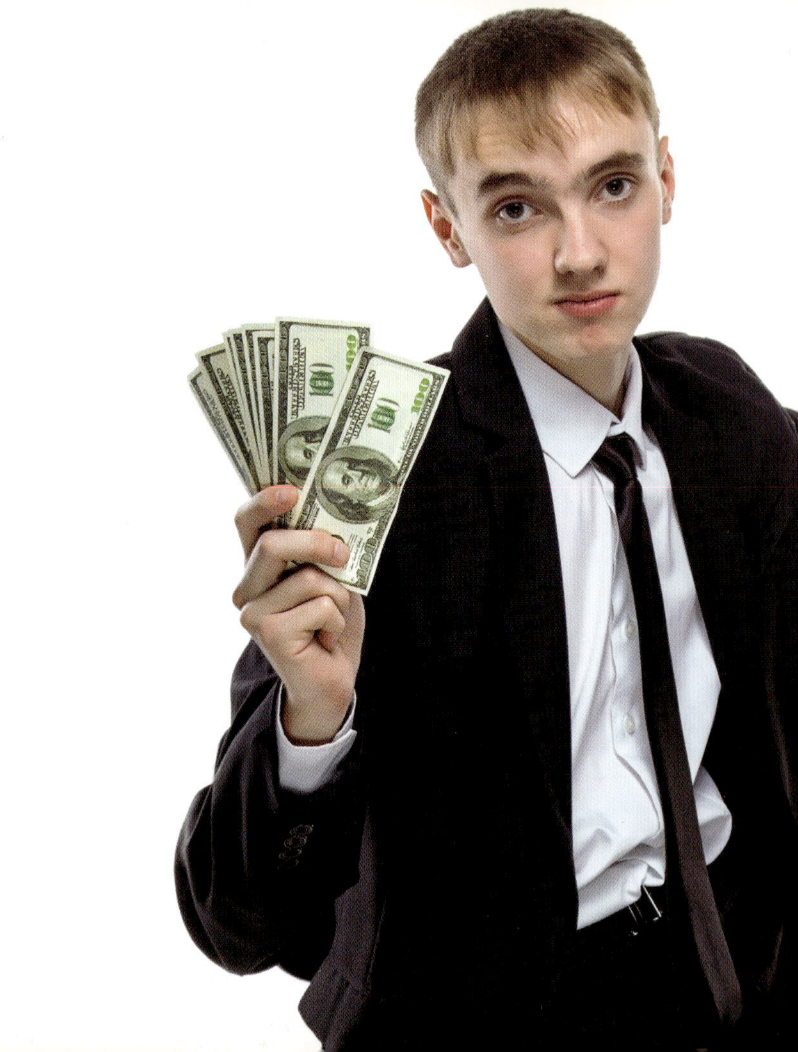
100

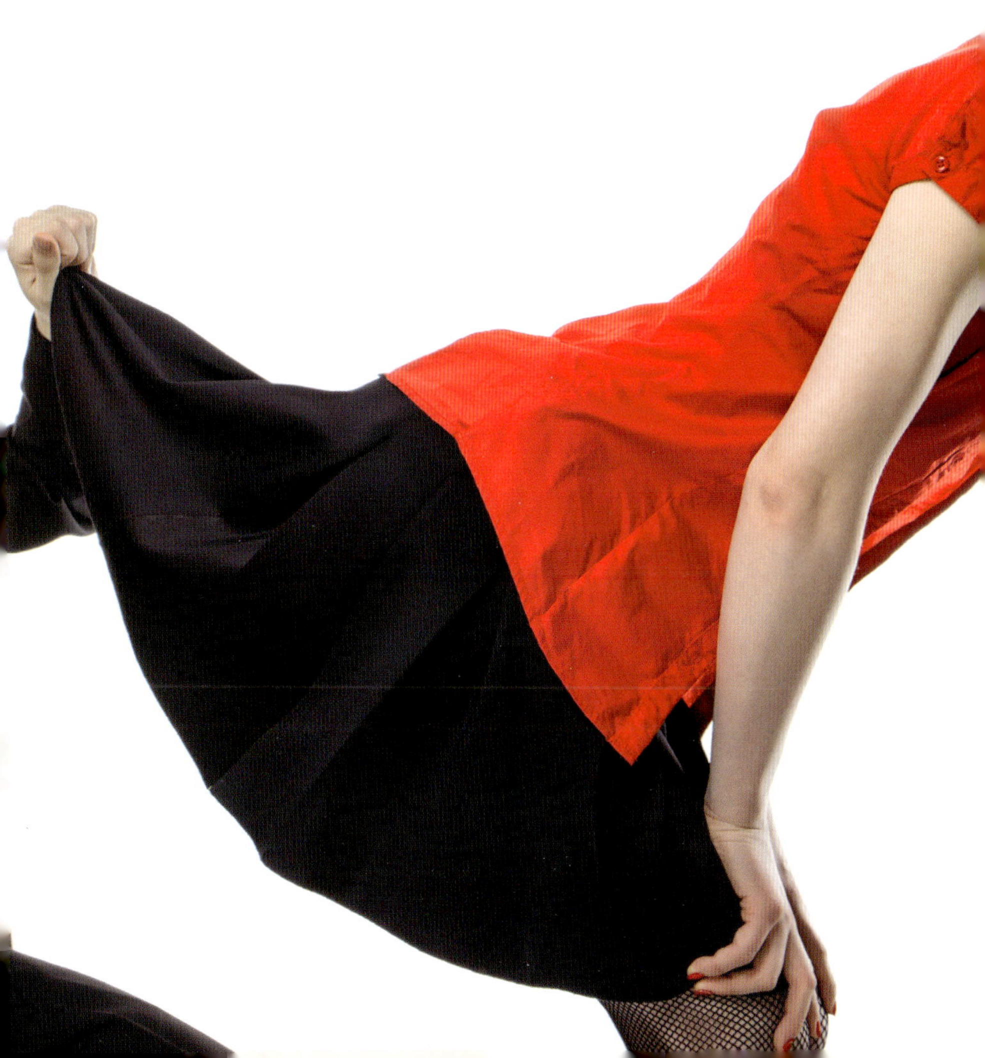

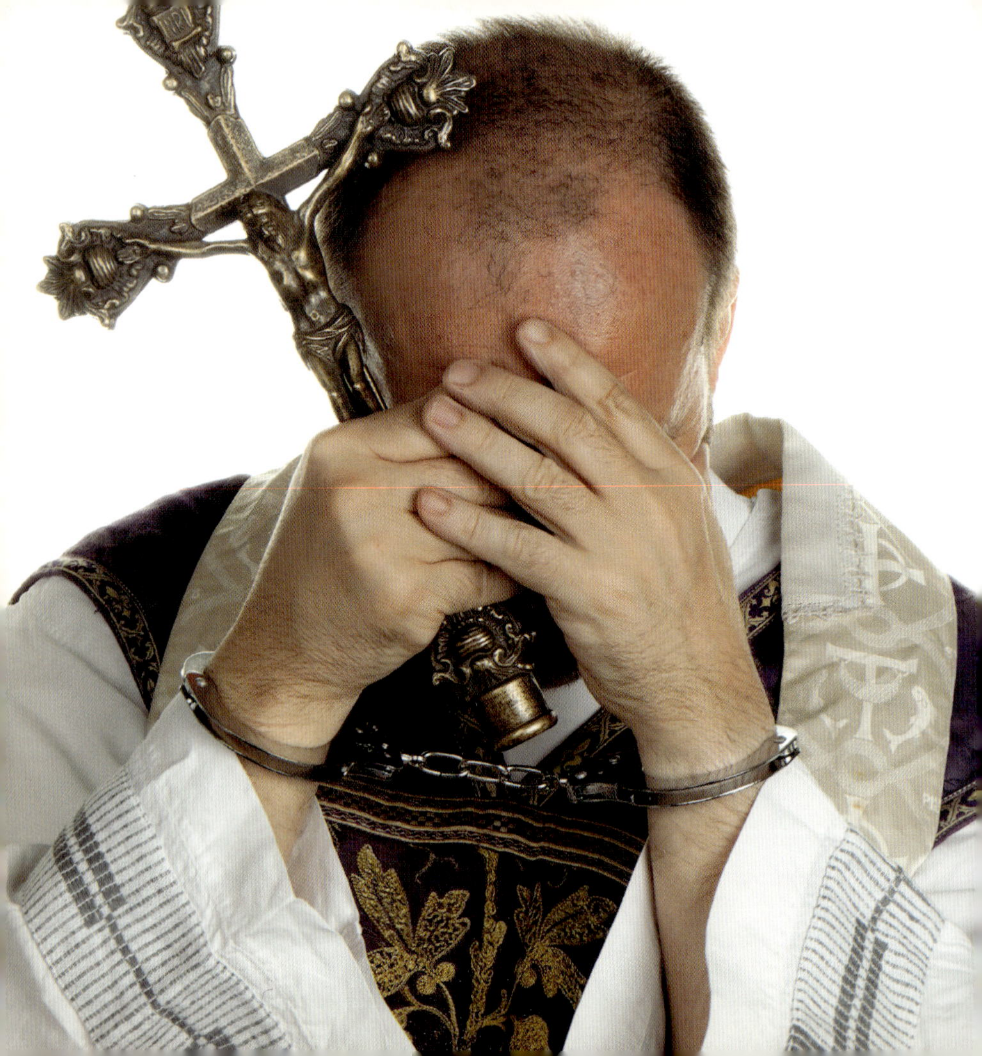

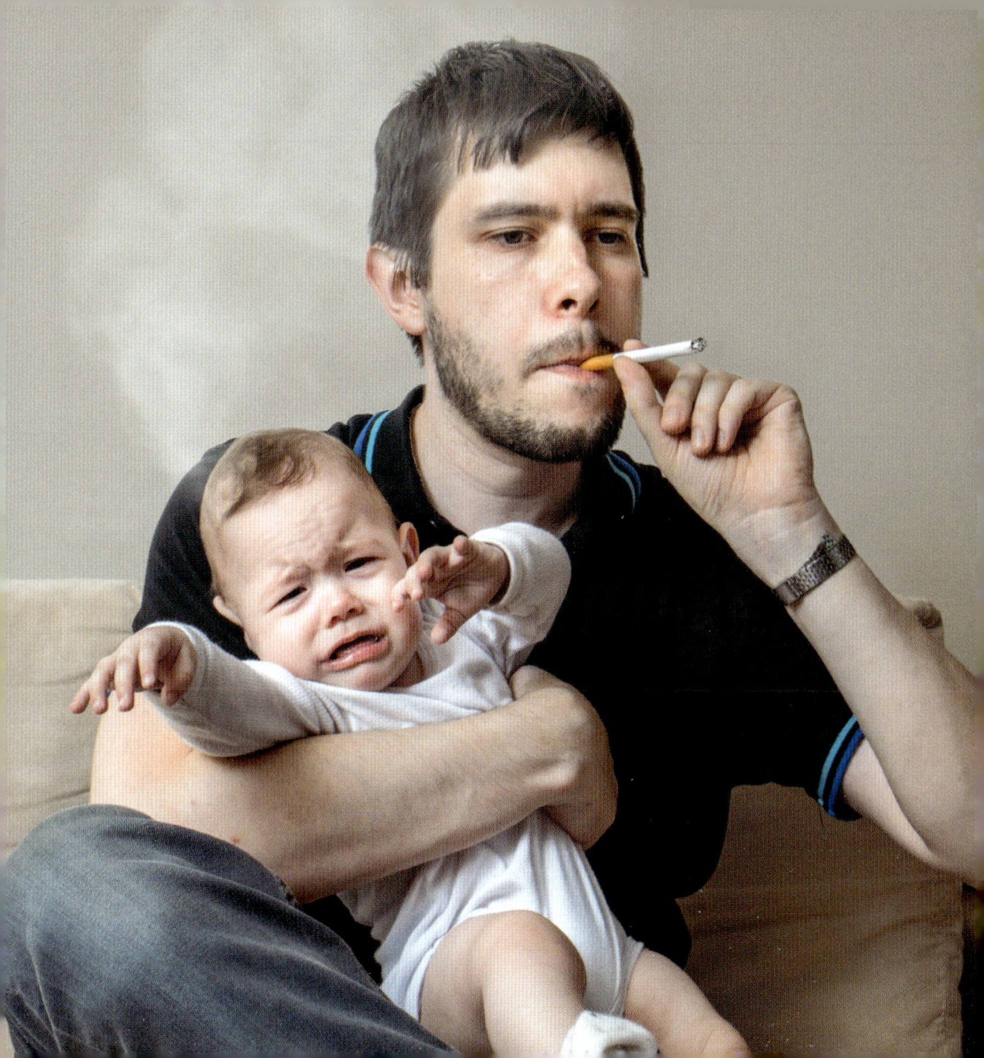

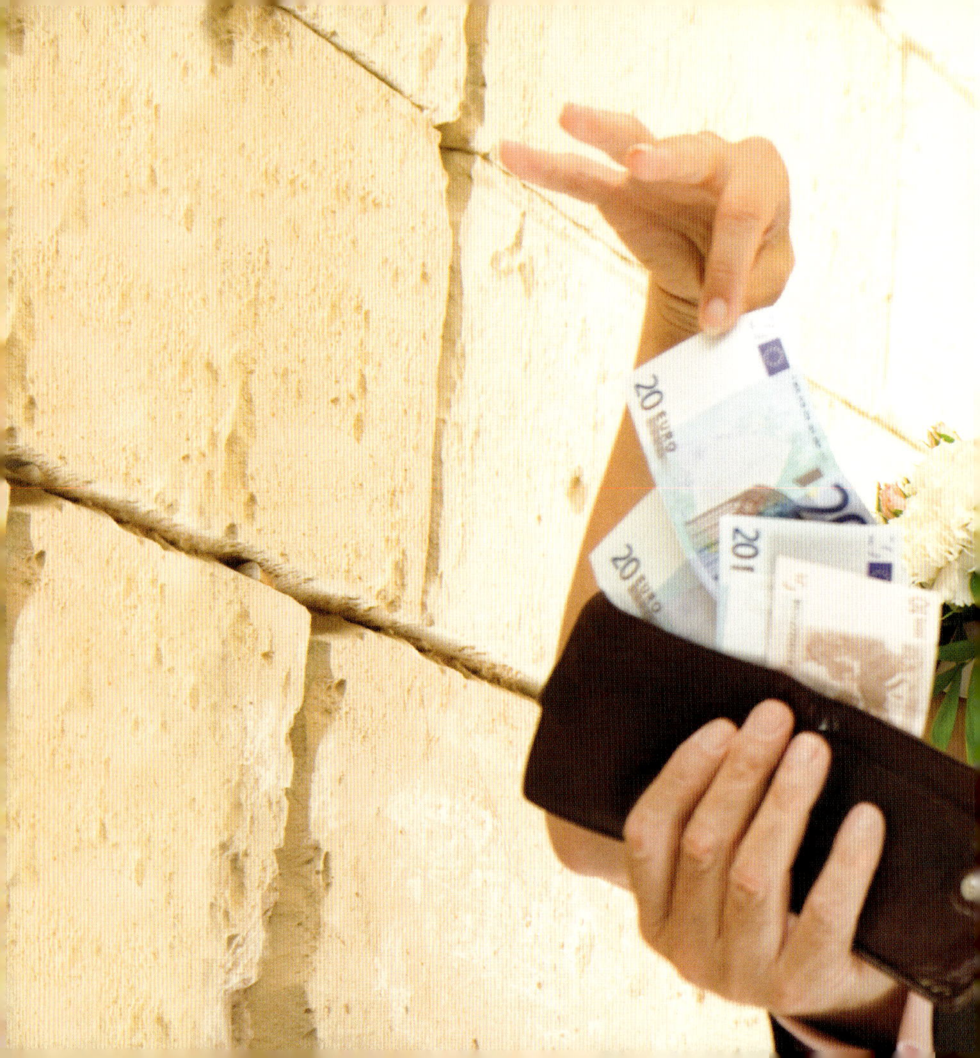
20 EURO
20 EURO

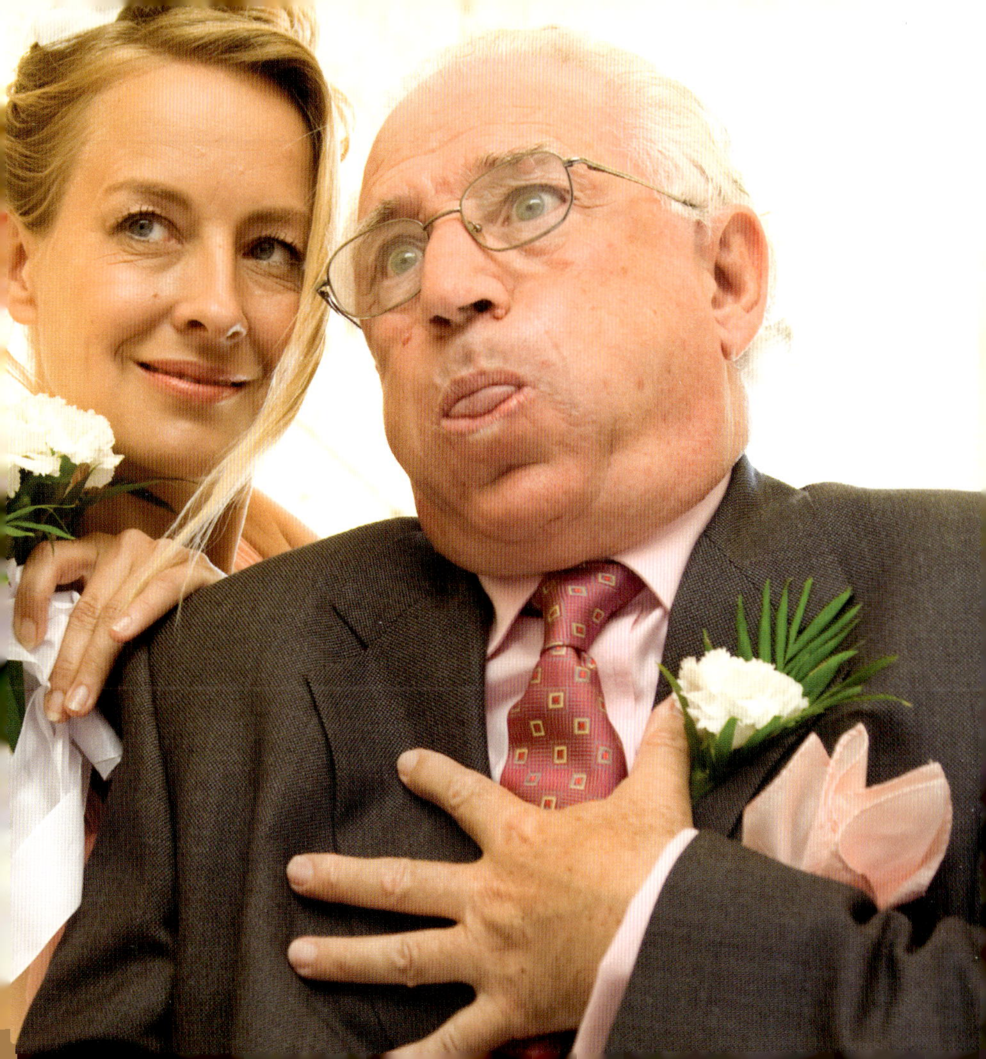

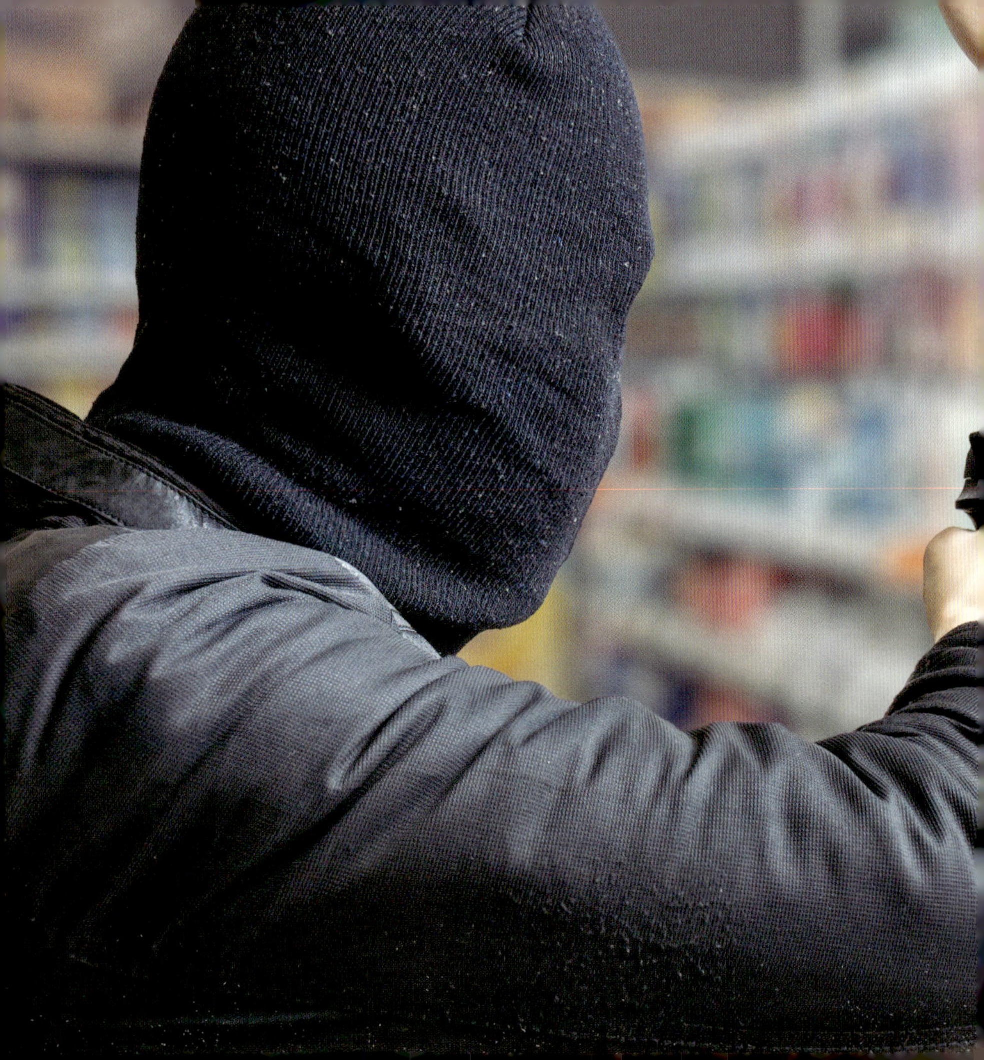

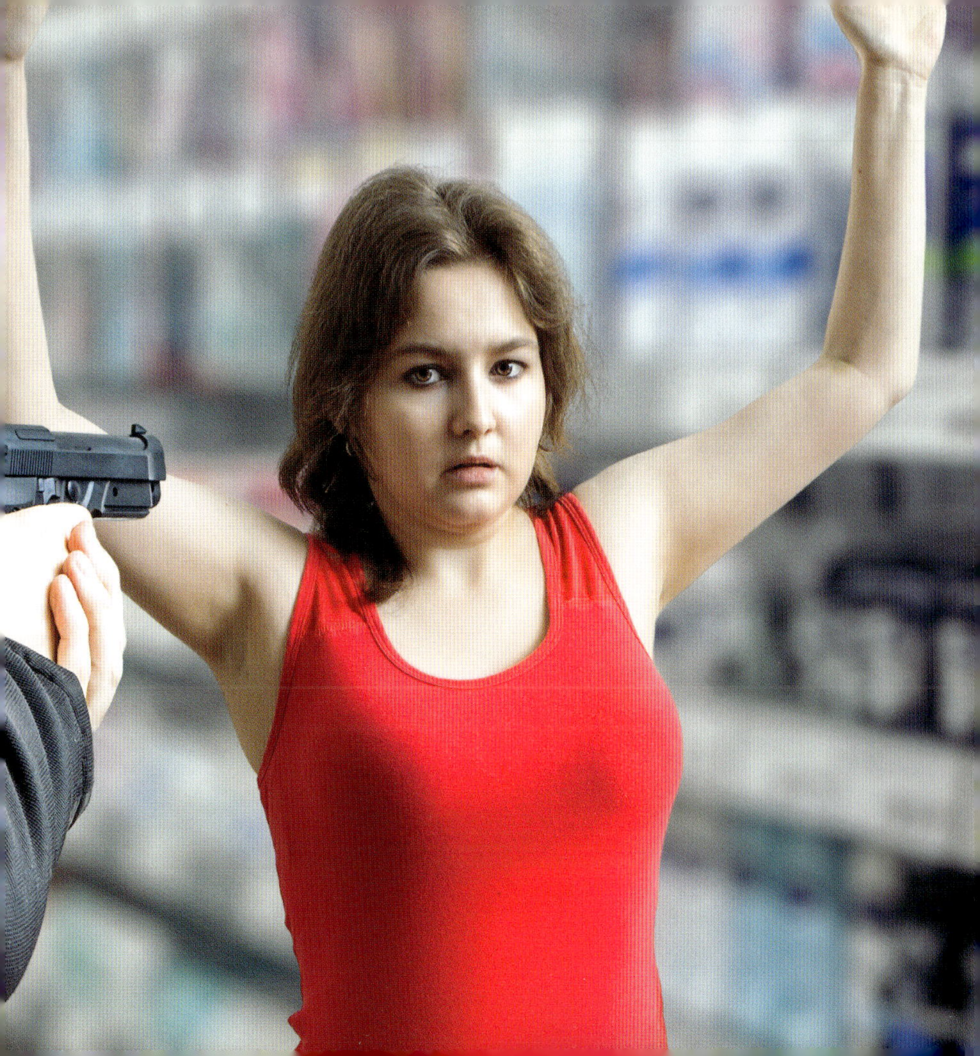

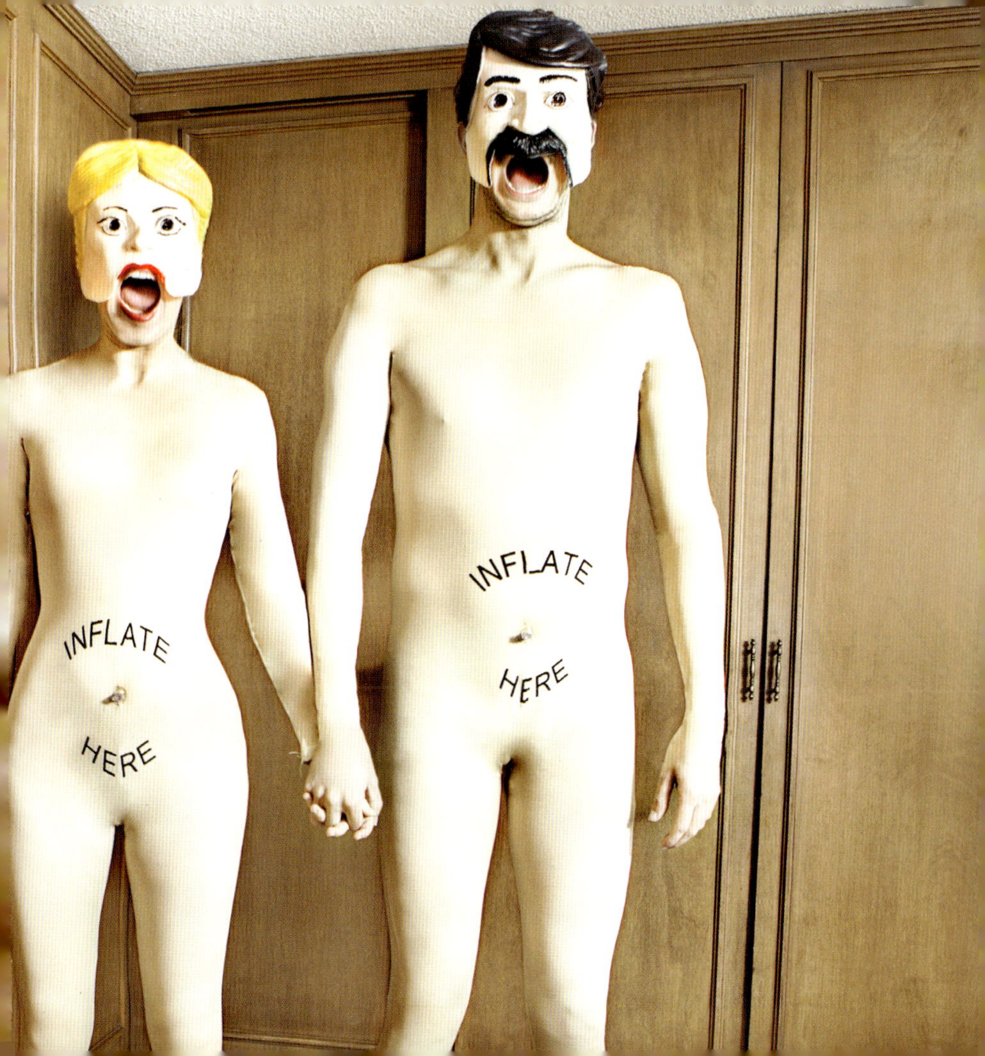
INFLATE
HERE
INFLATE
HERE

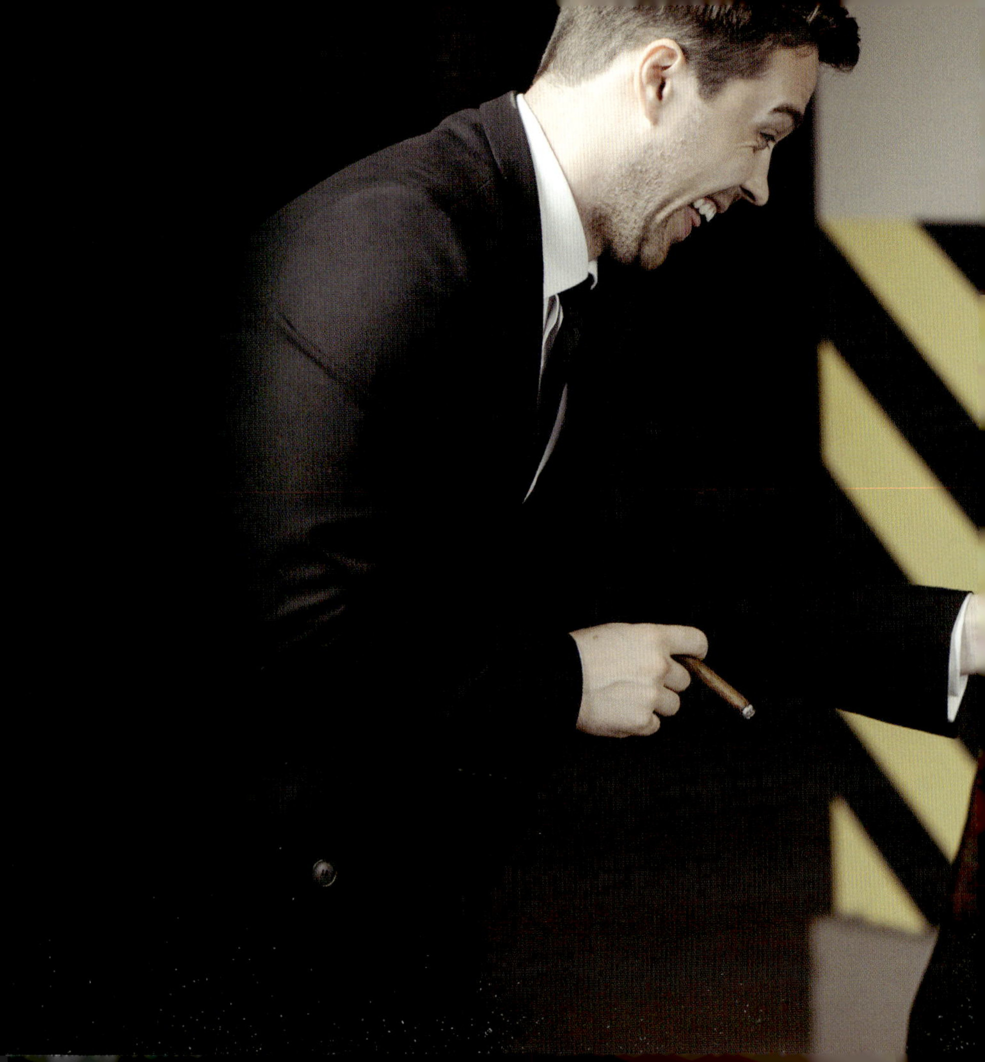

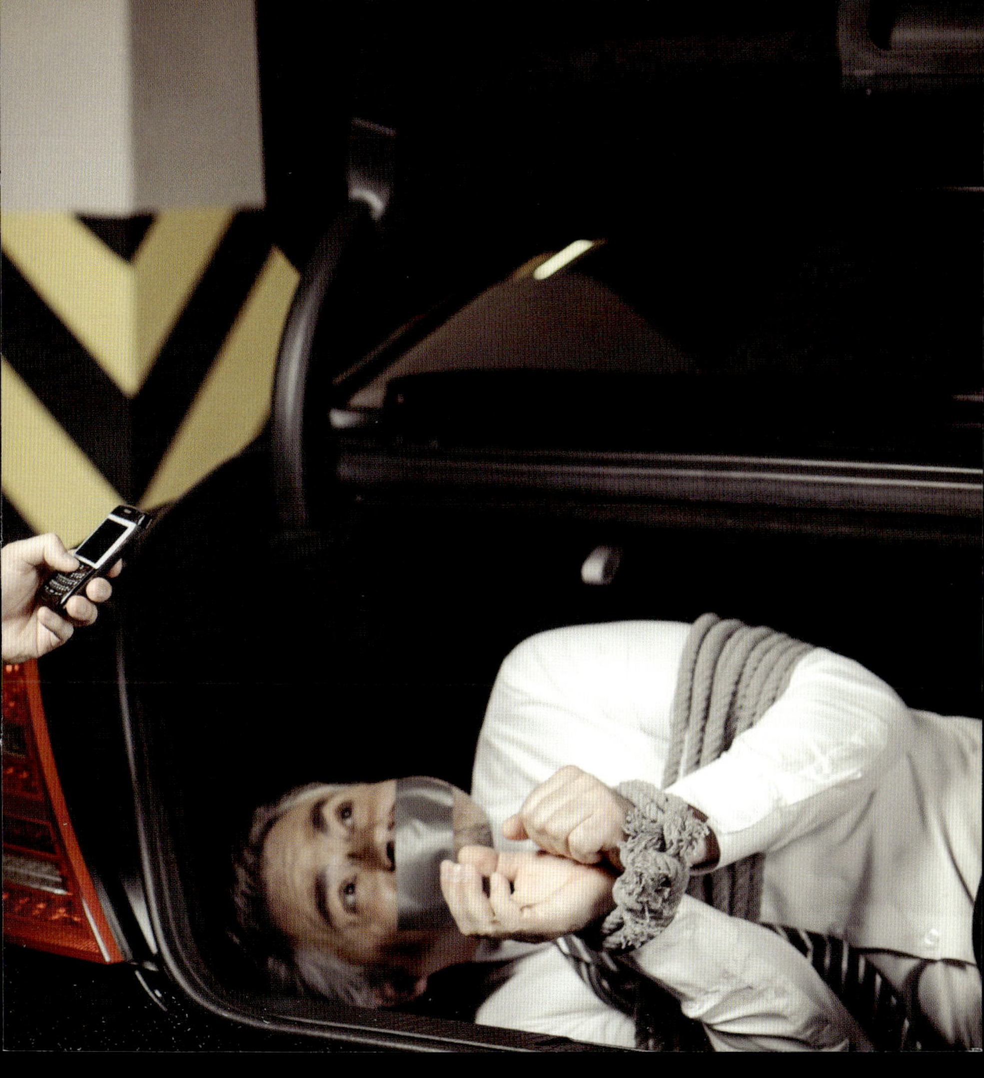

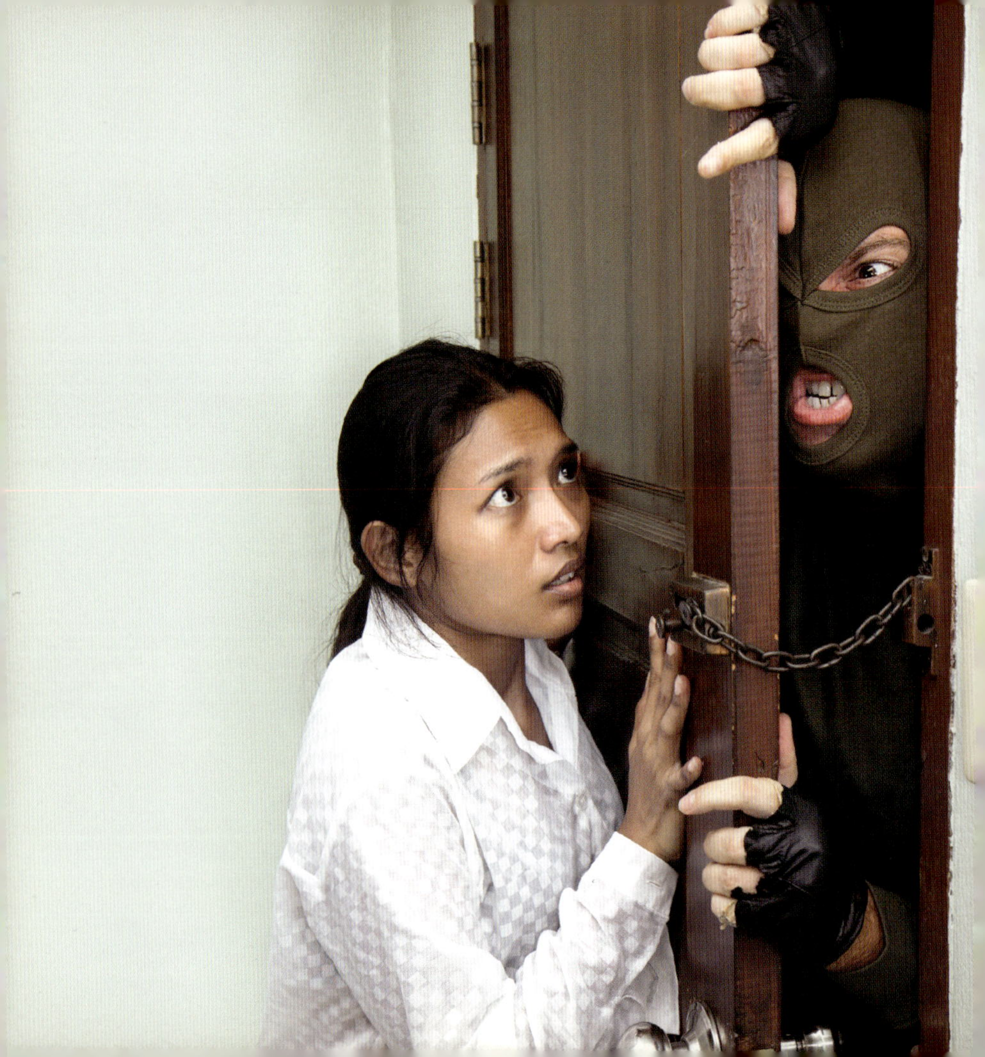

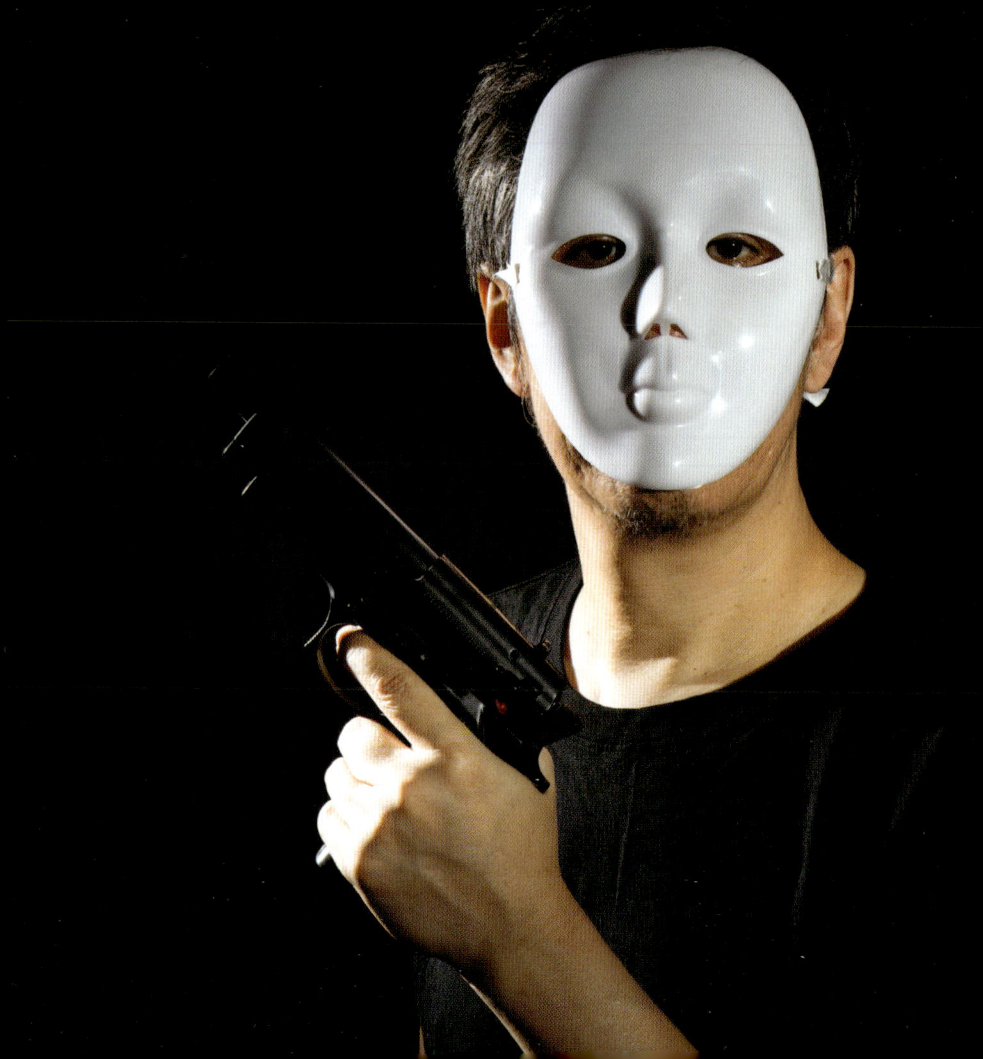

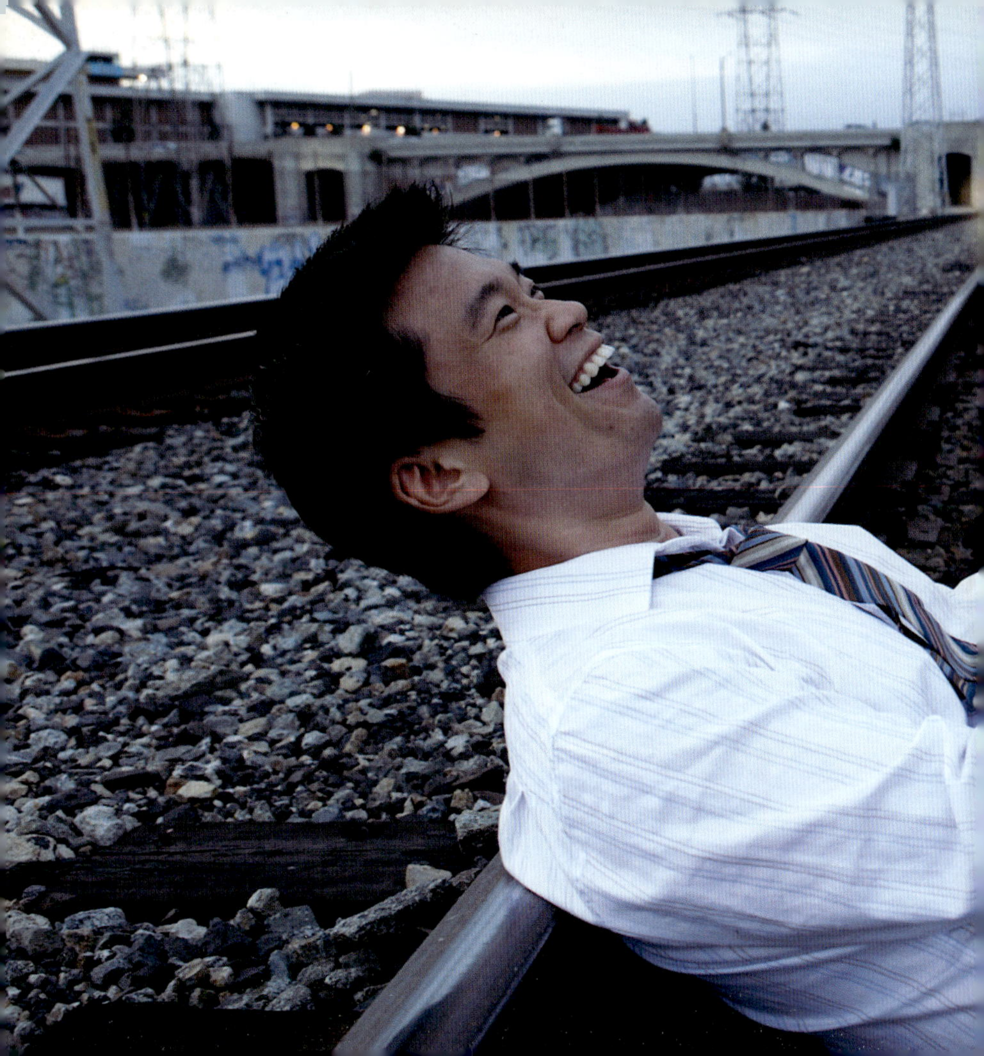

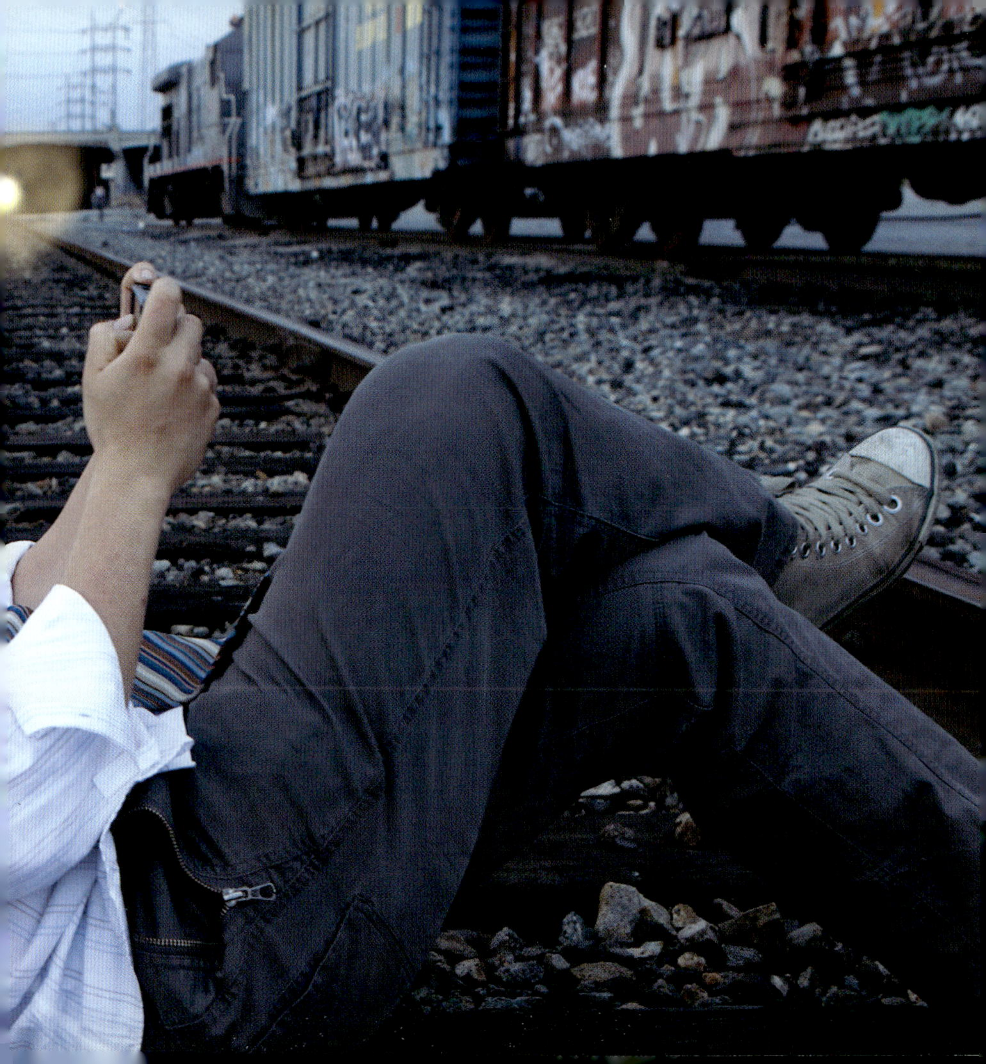

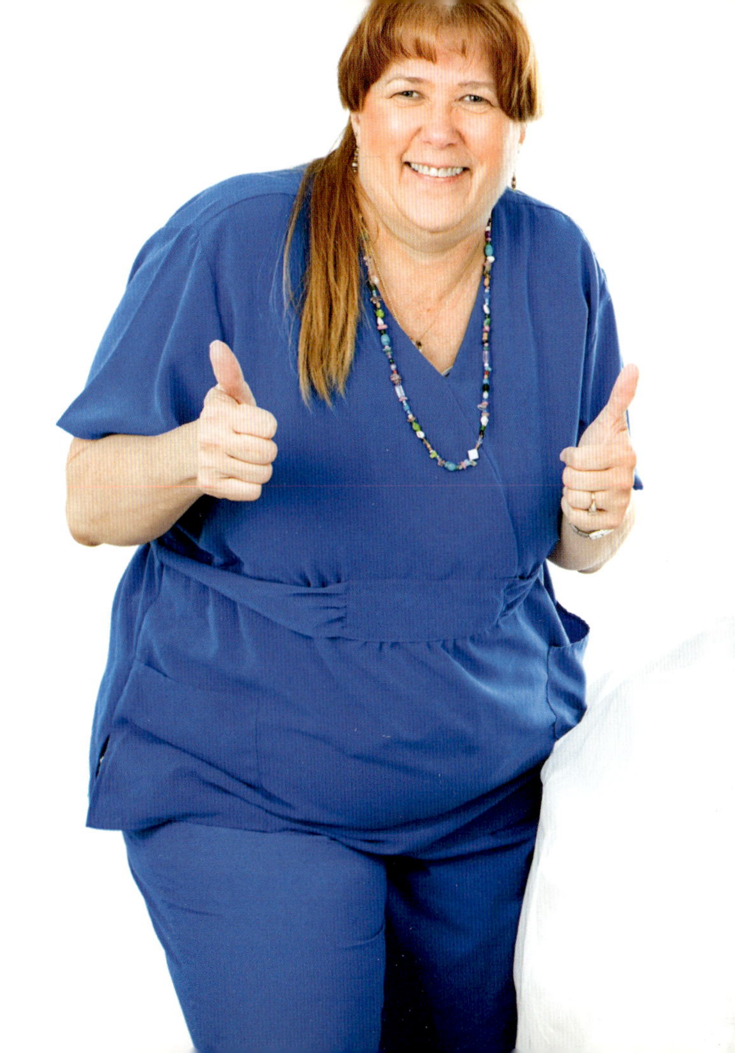

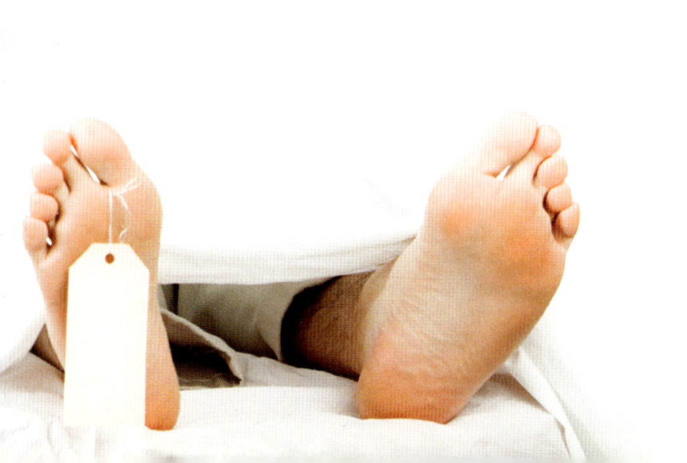

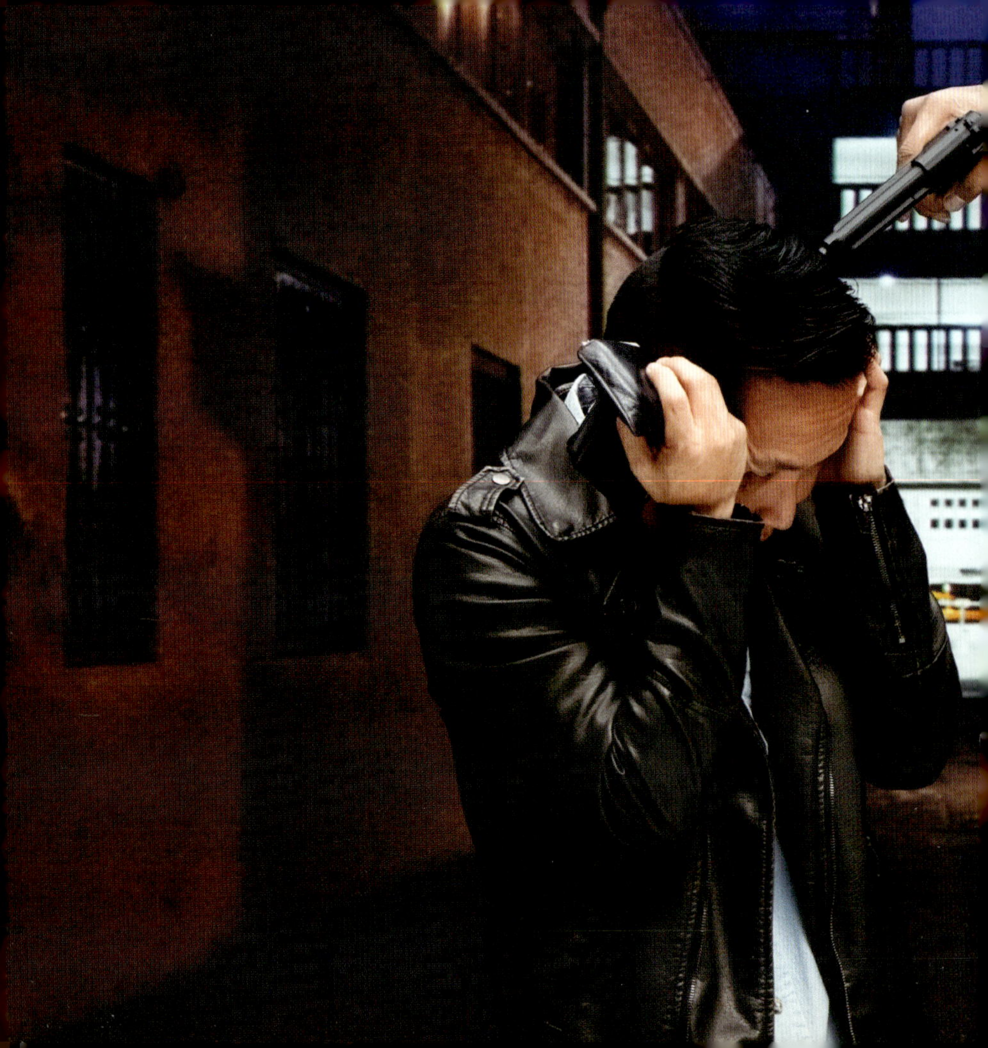

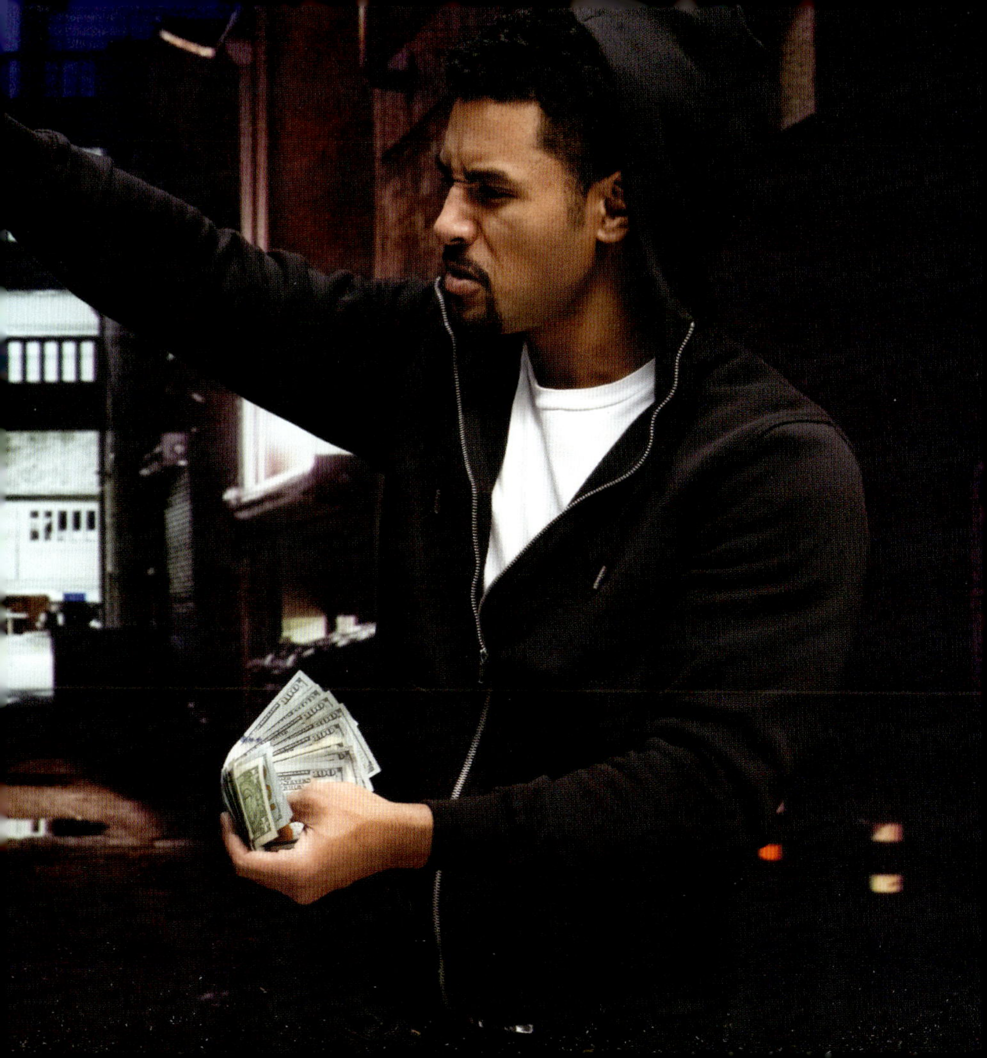

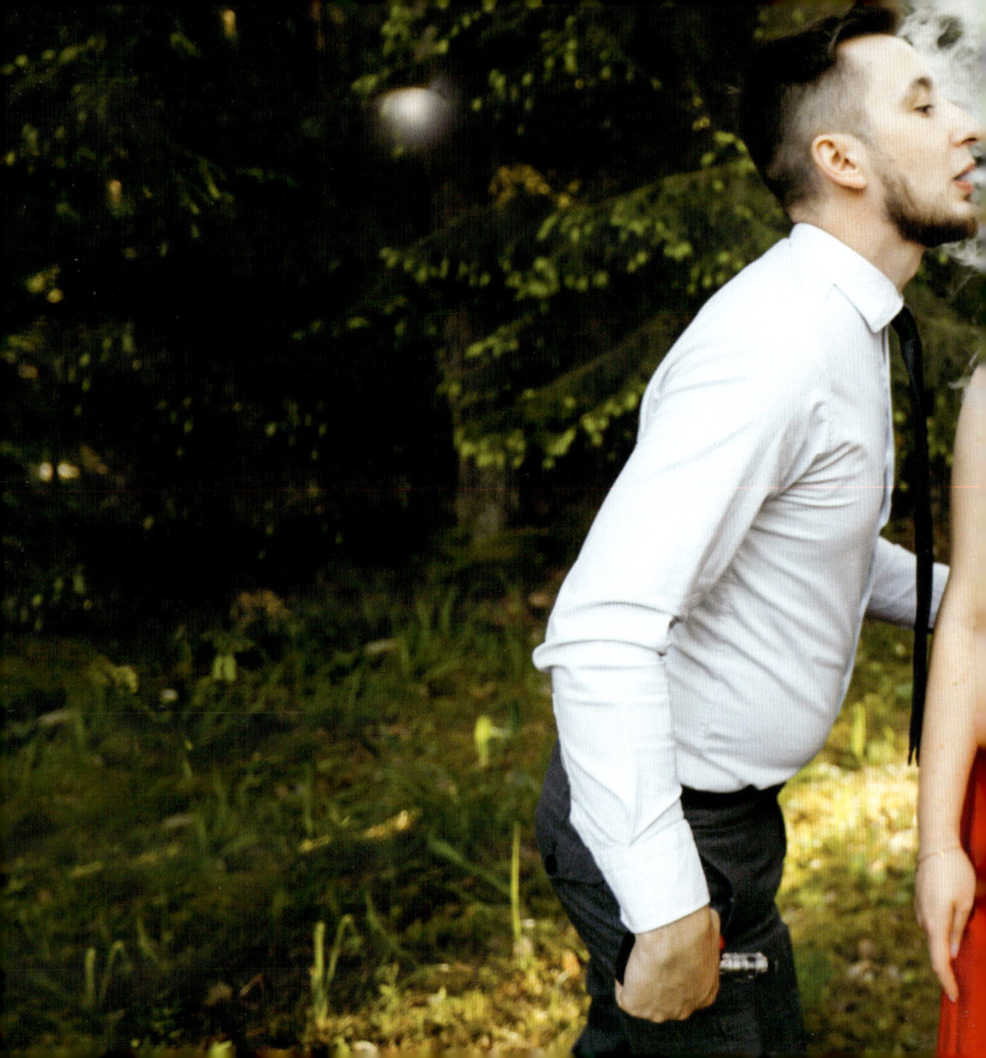

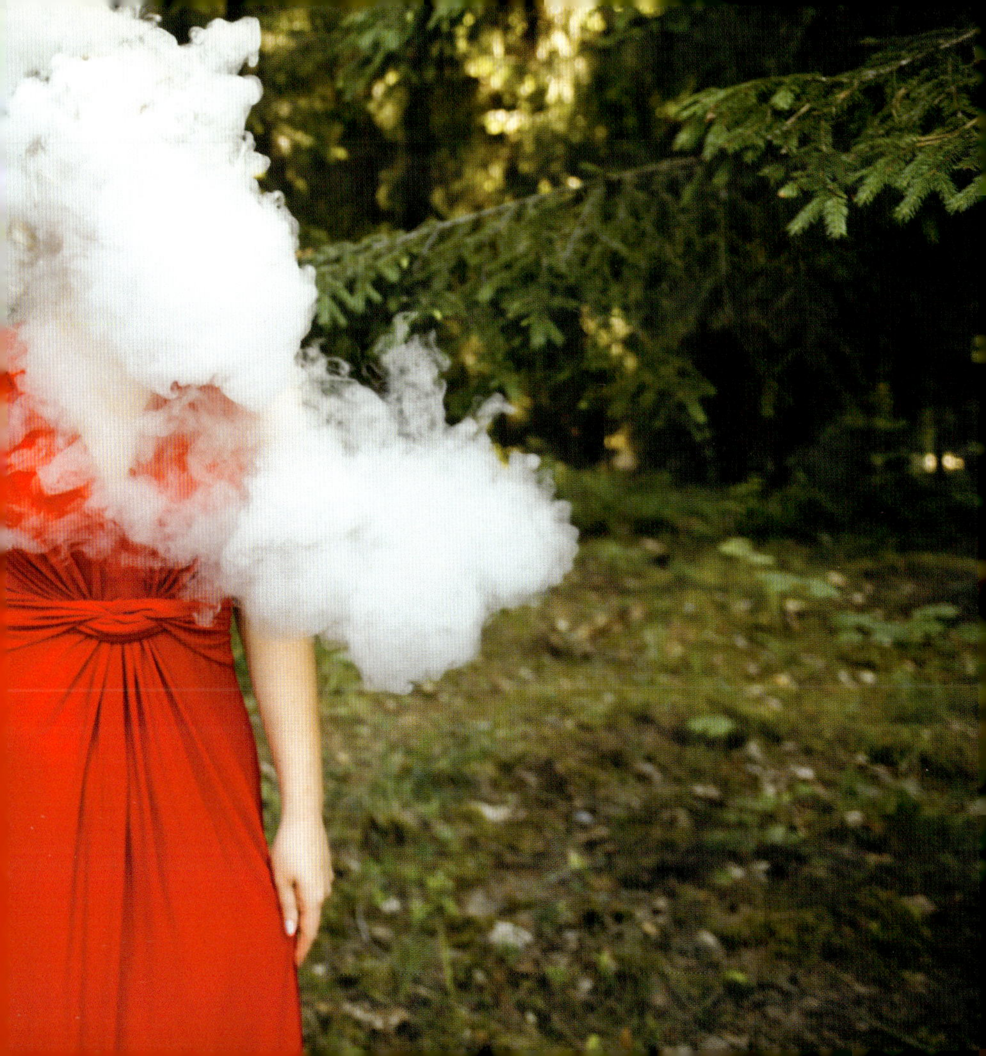

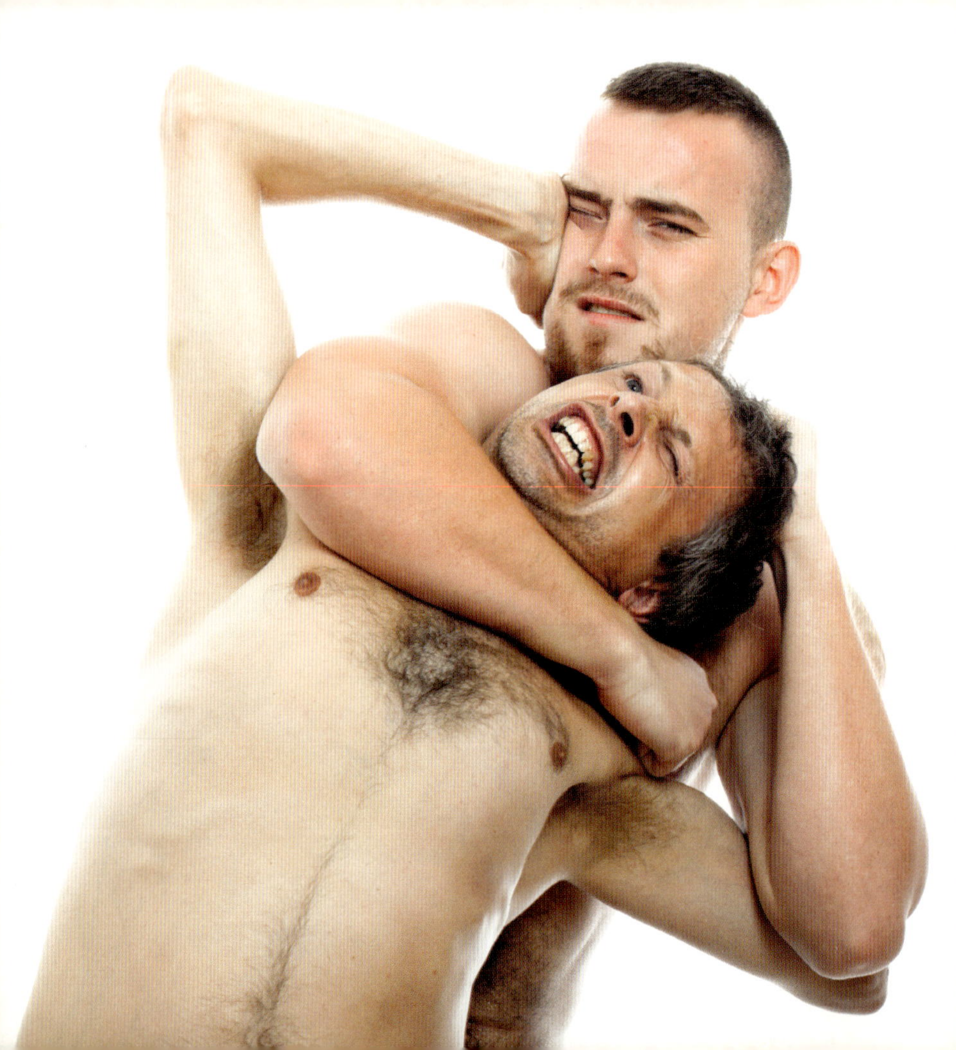

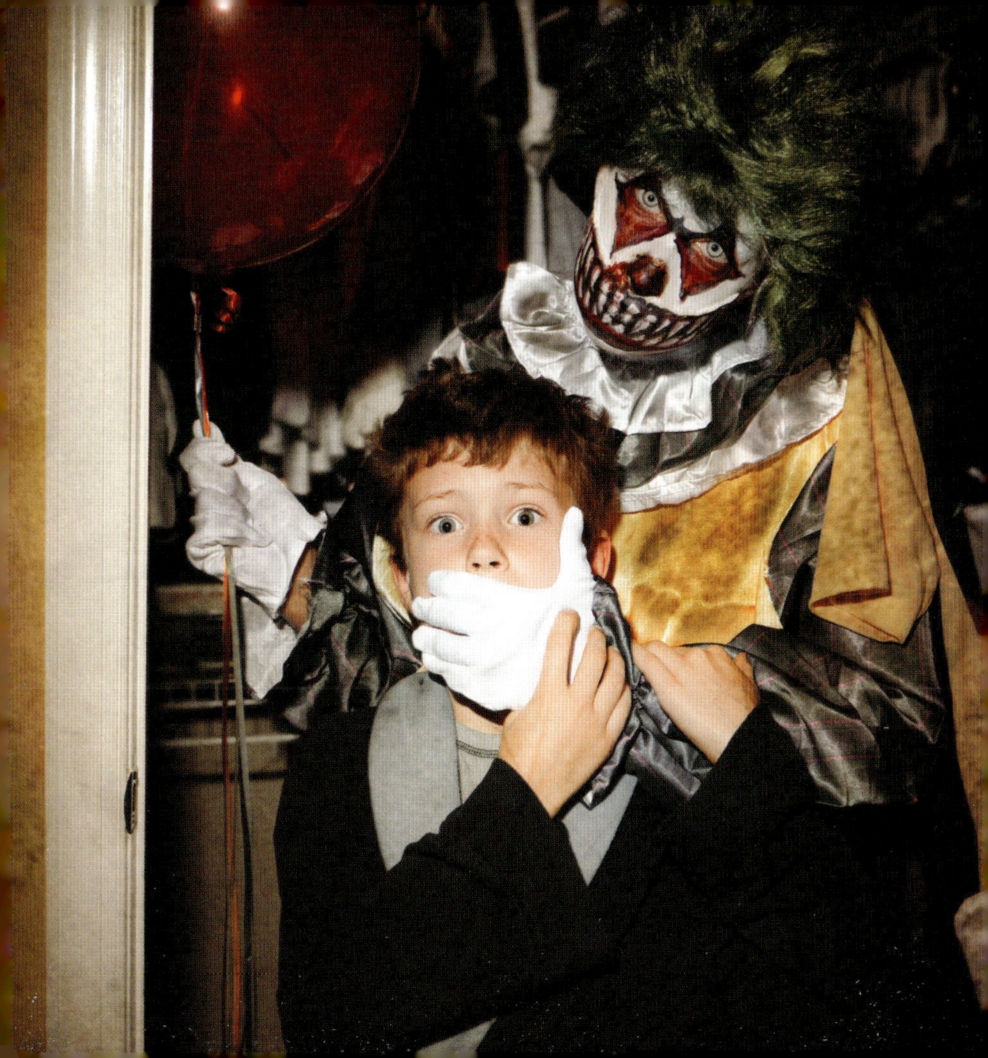

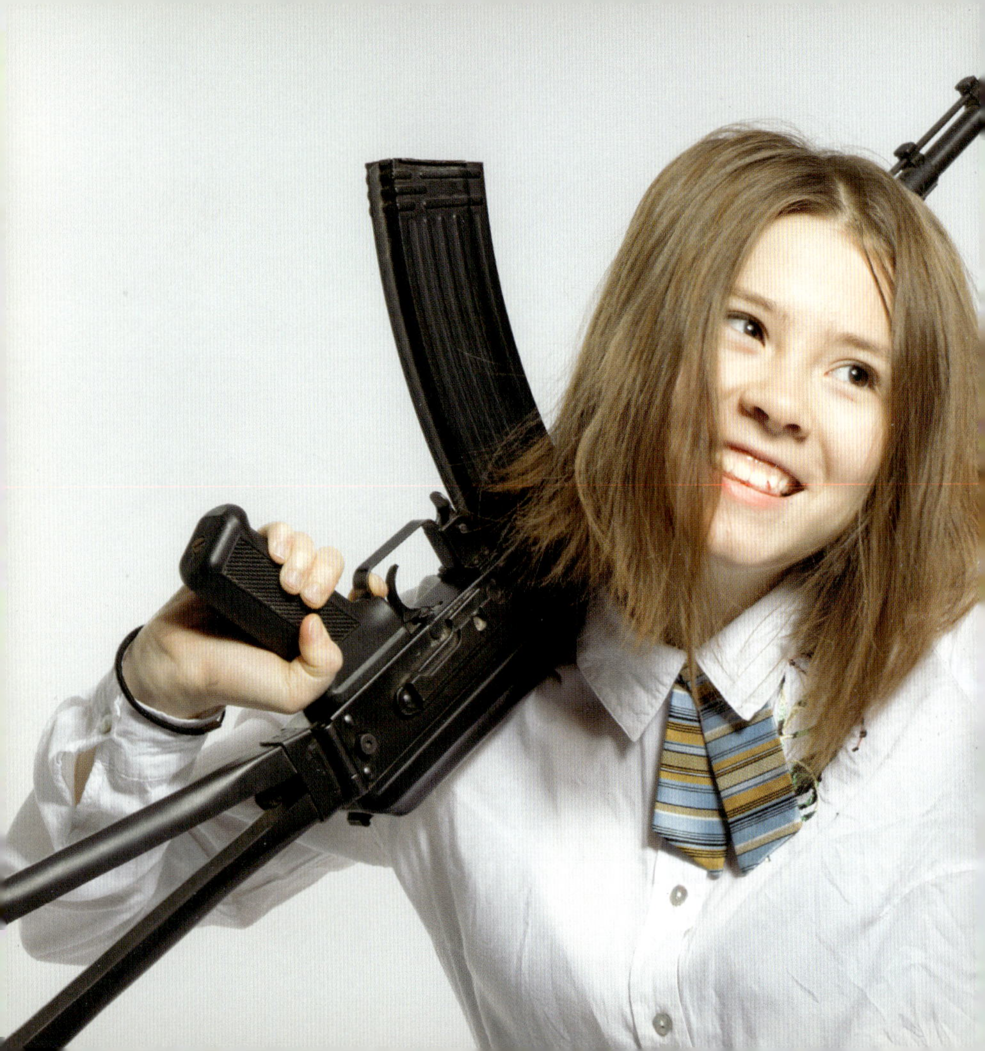

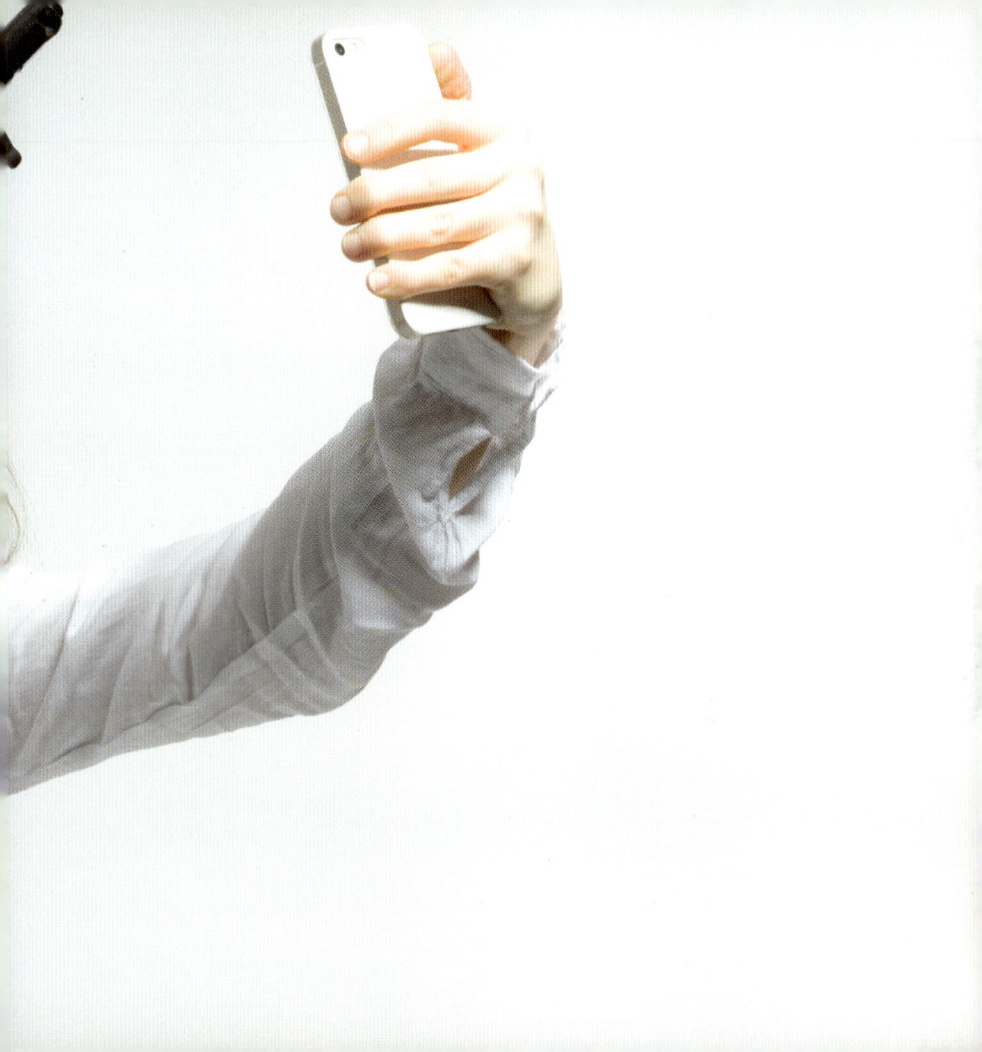

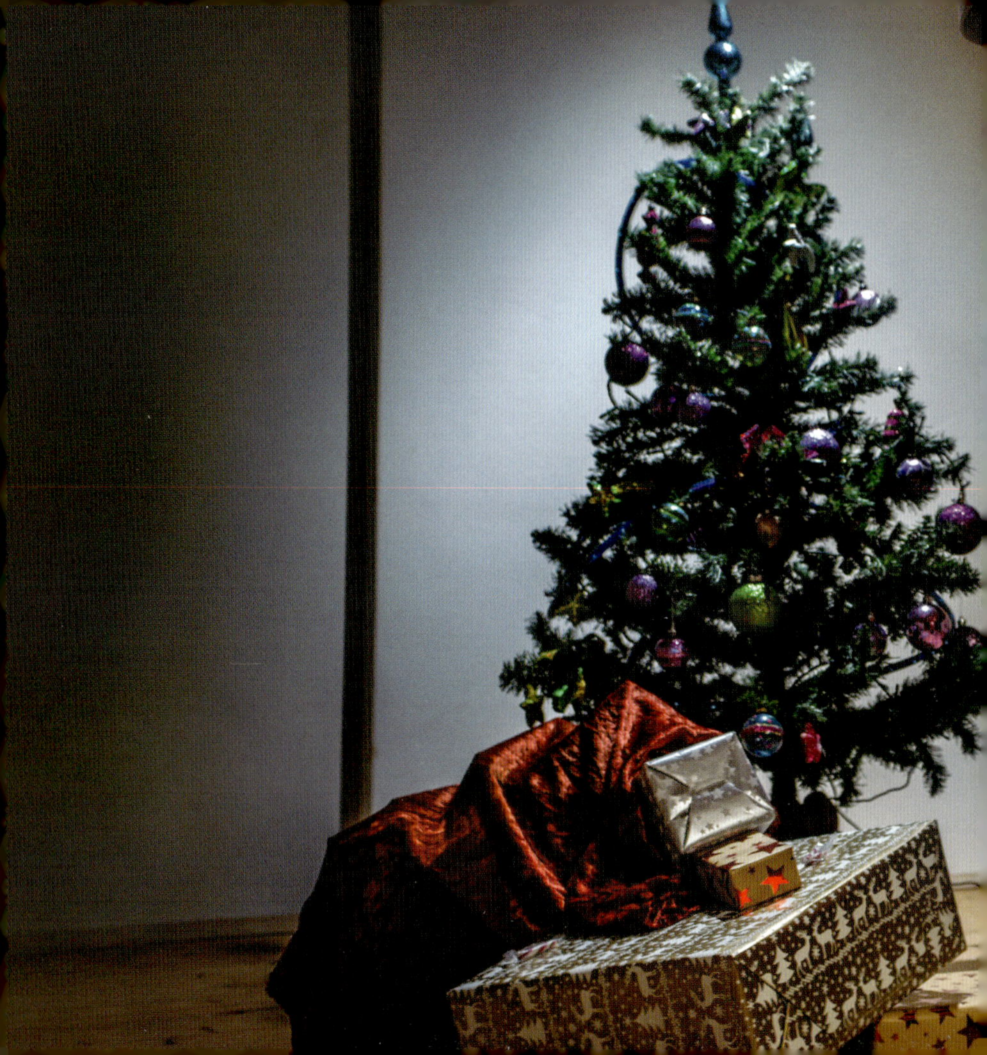

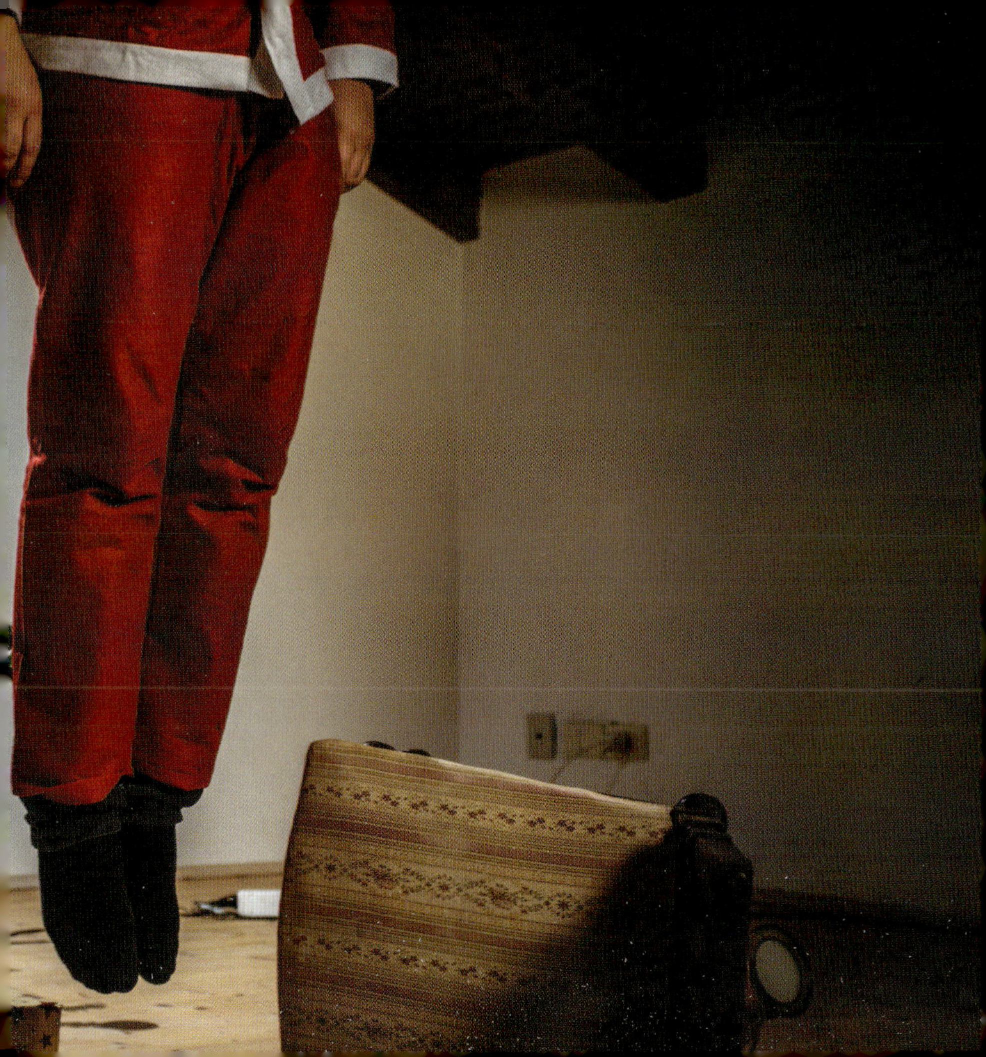

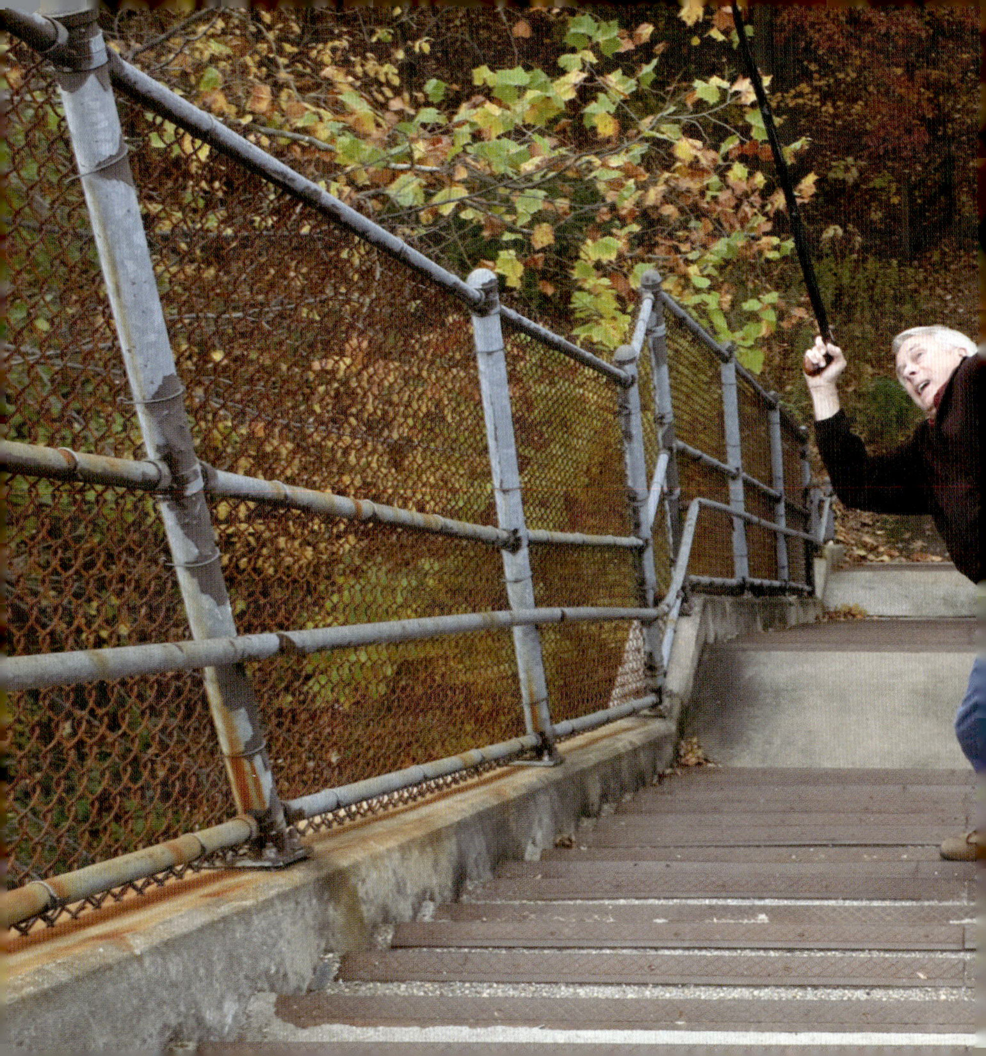

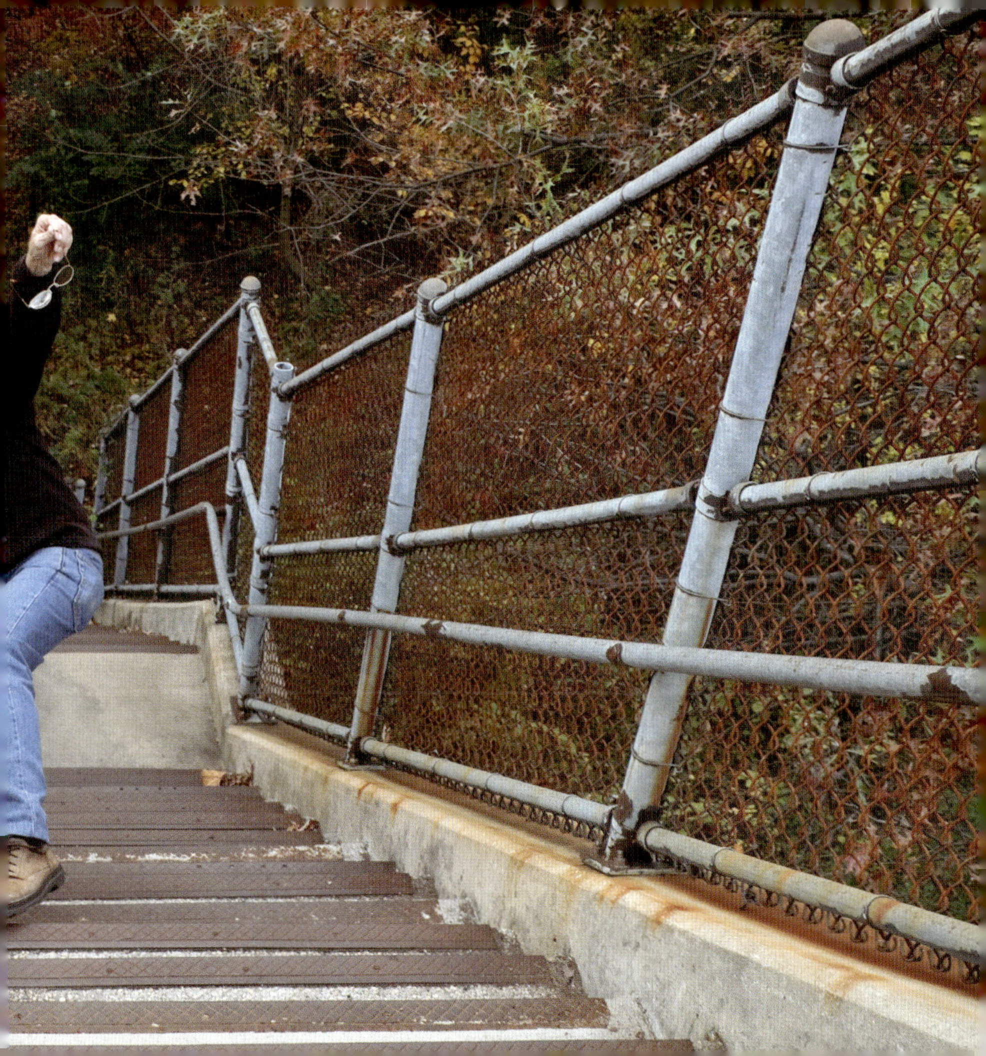

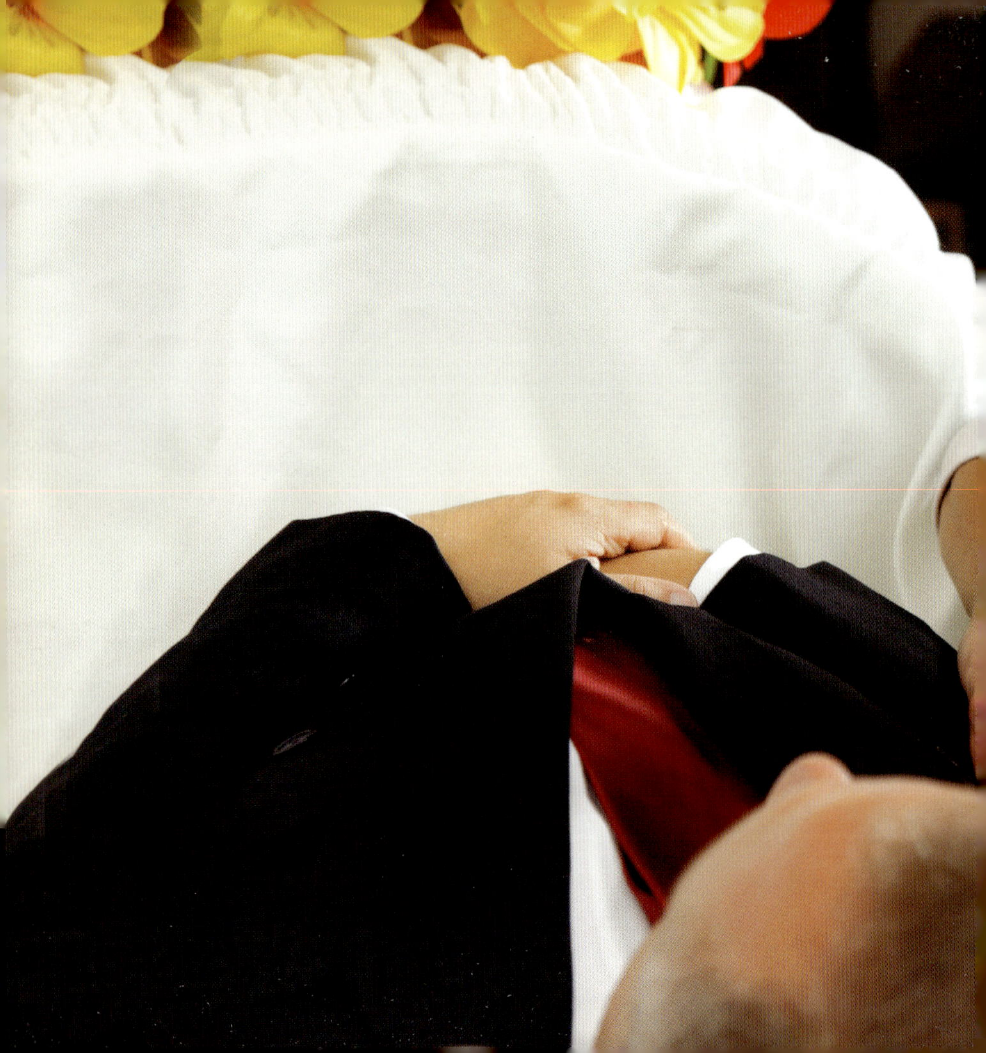

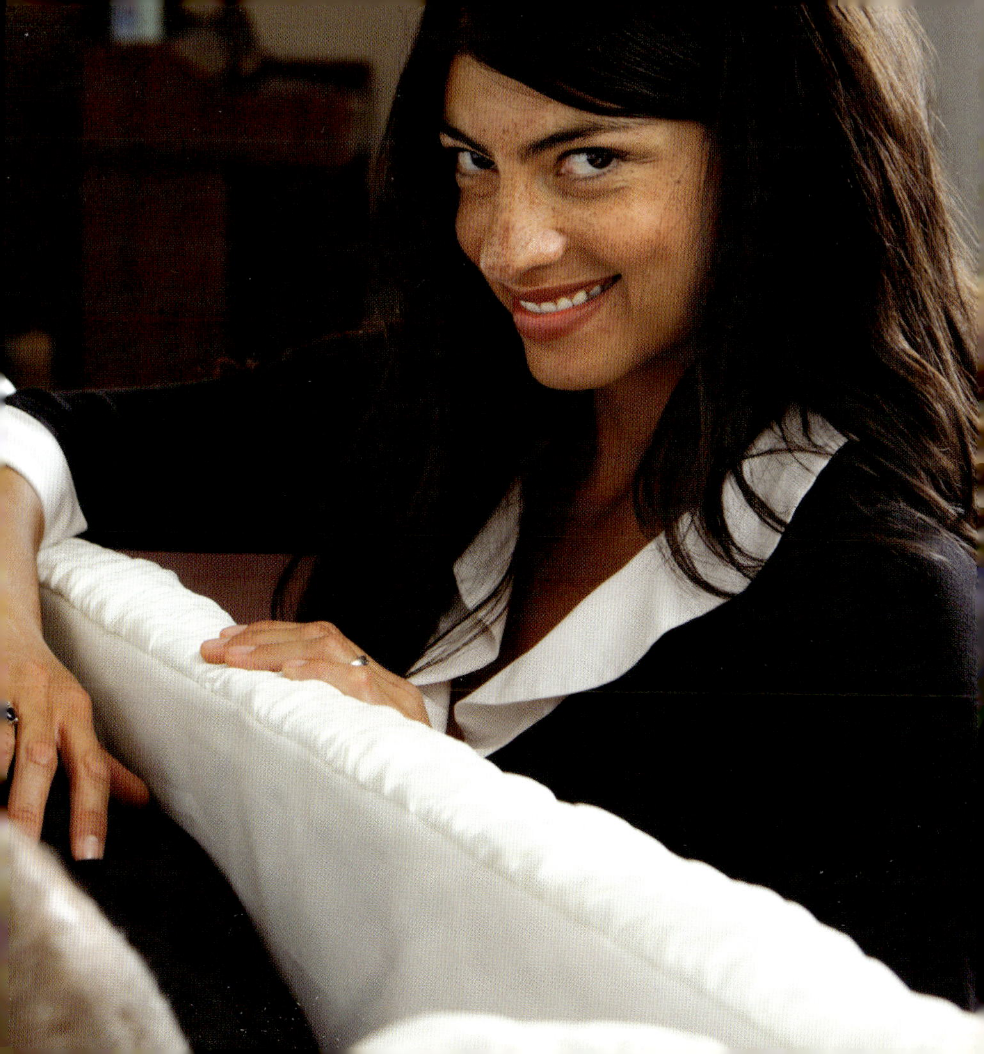

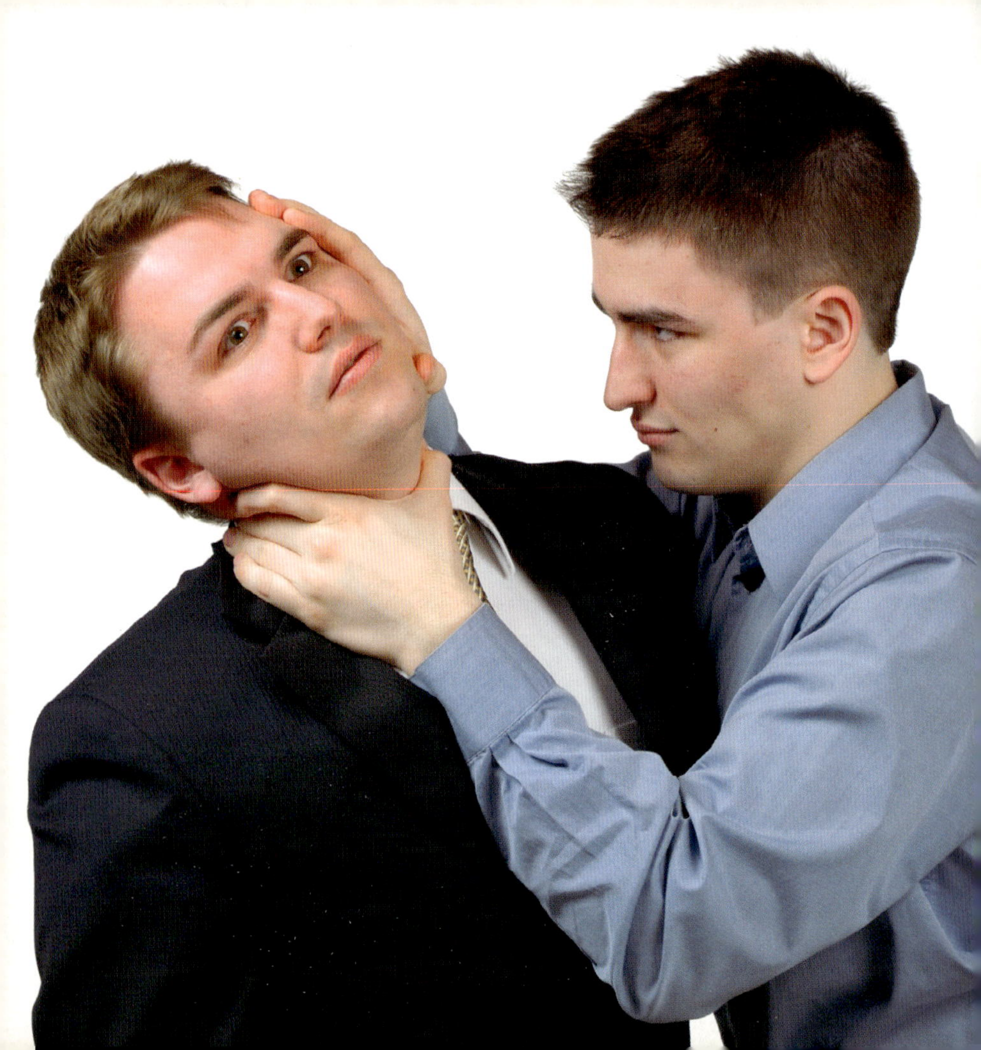

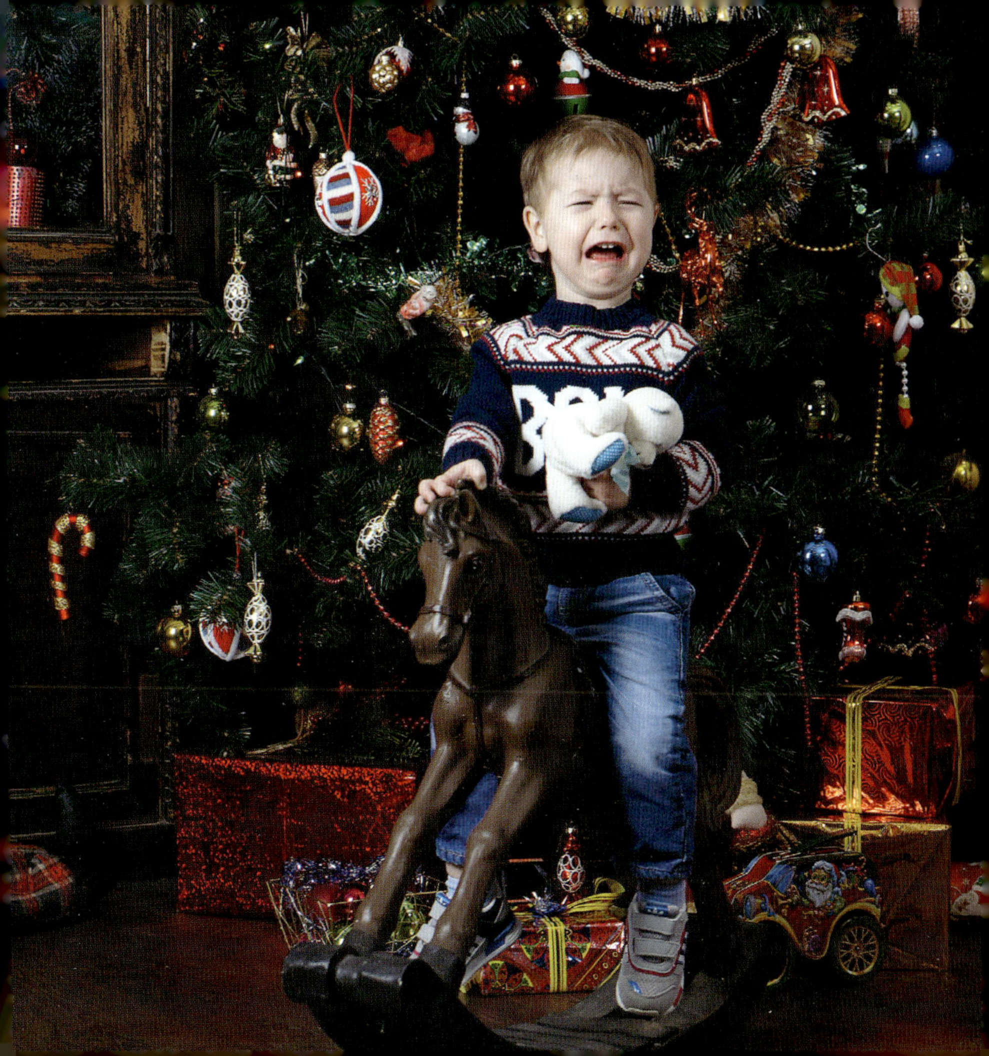

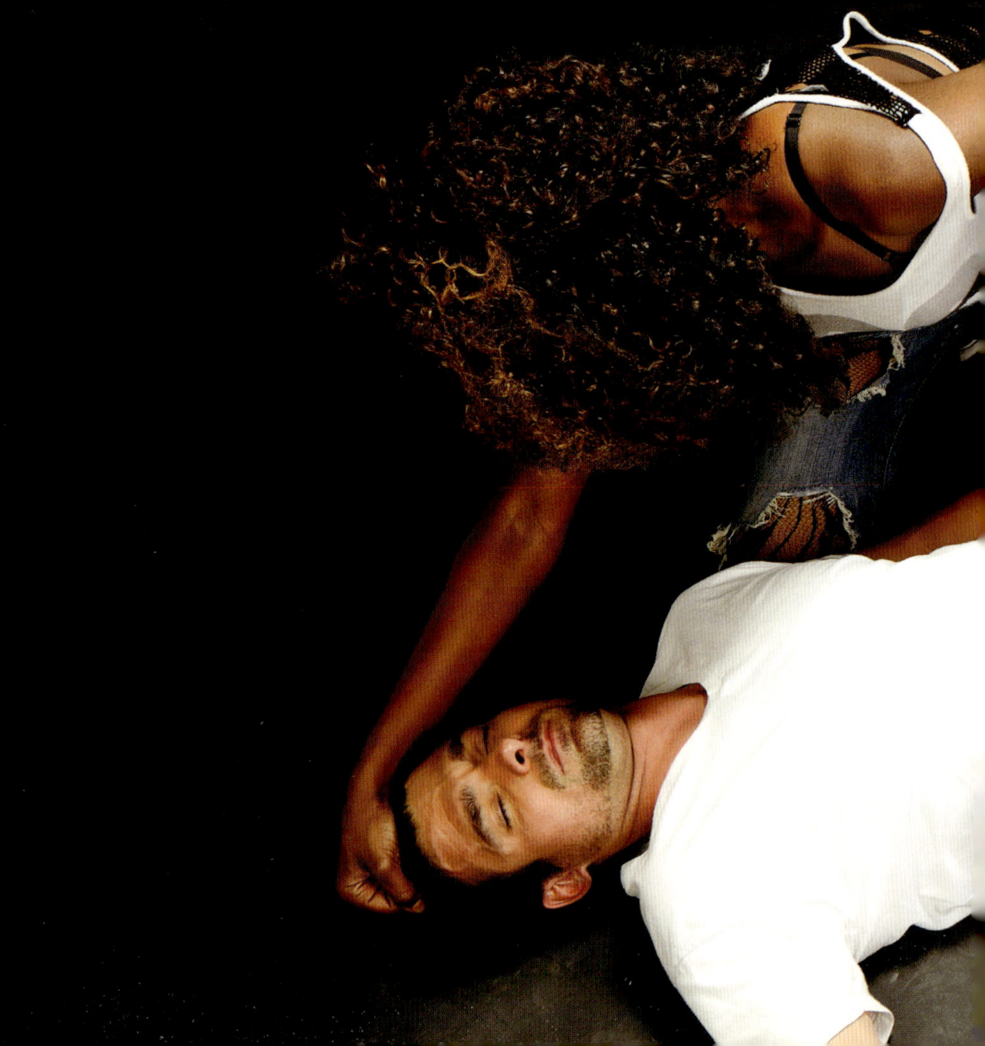

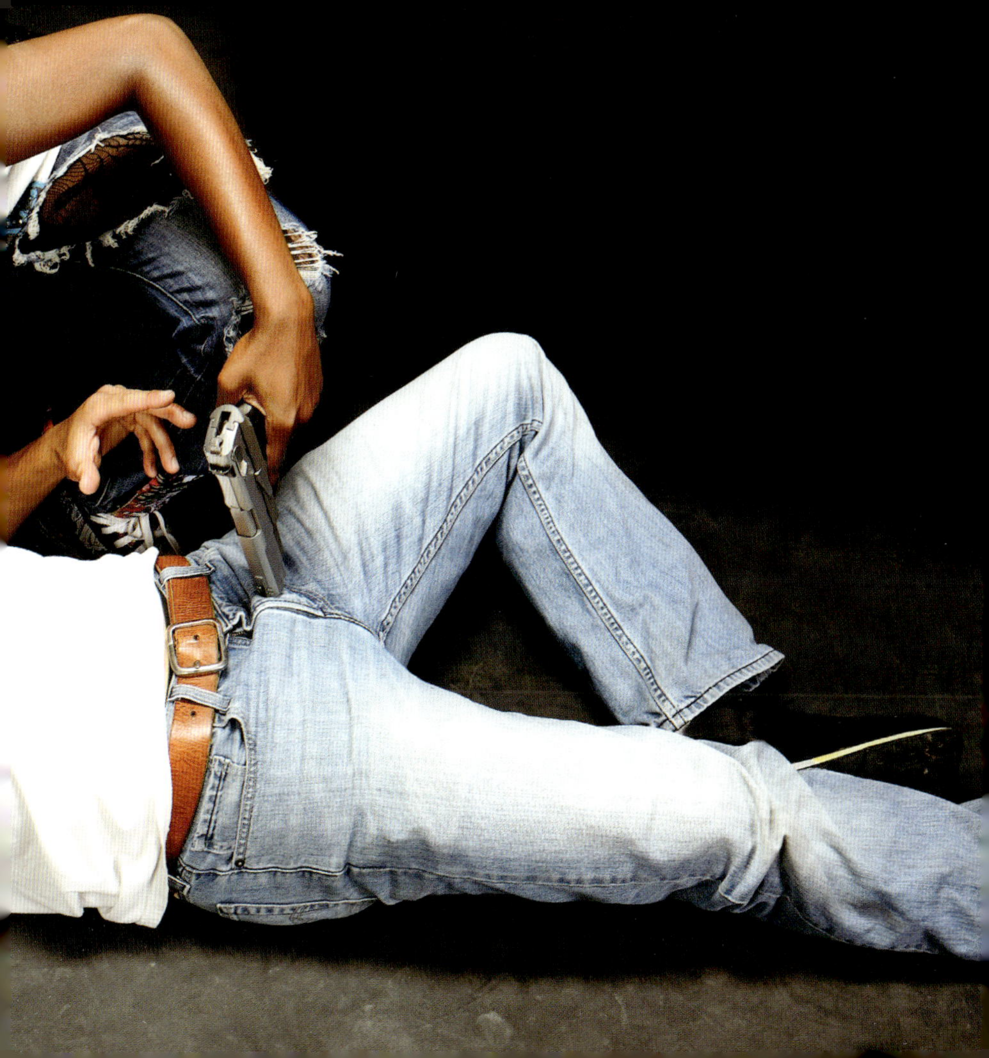

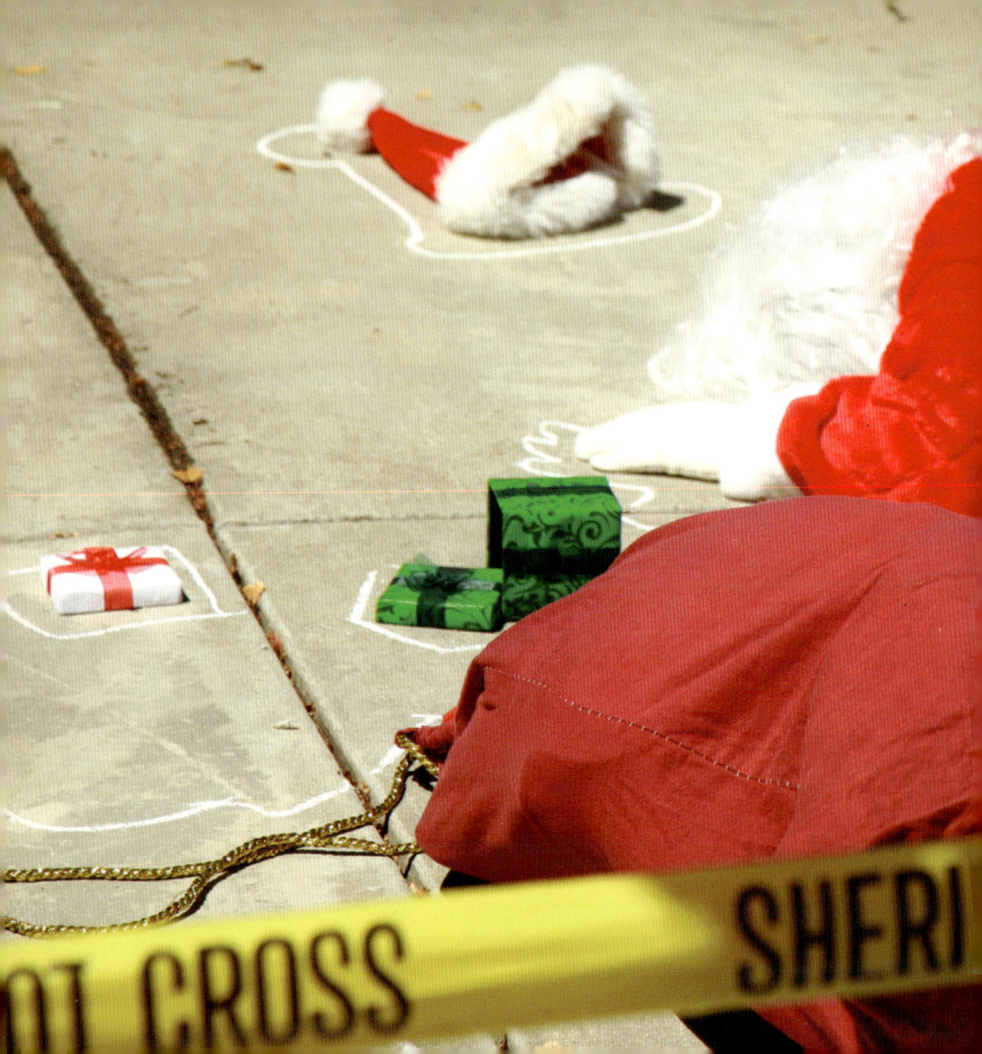
CROSS
SHERI

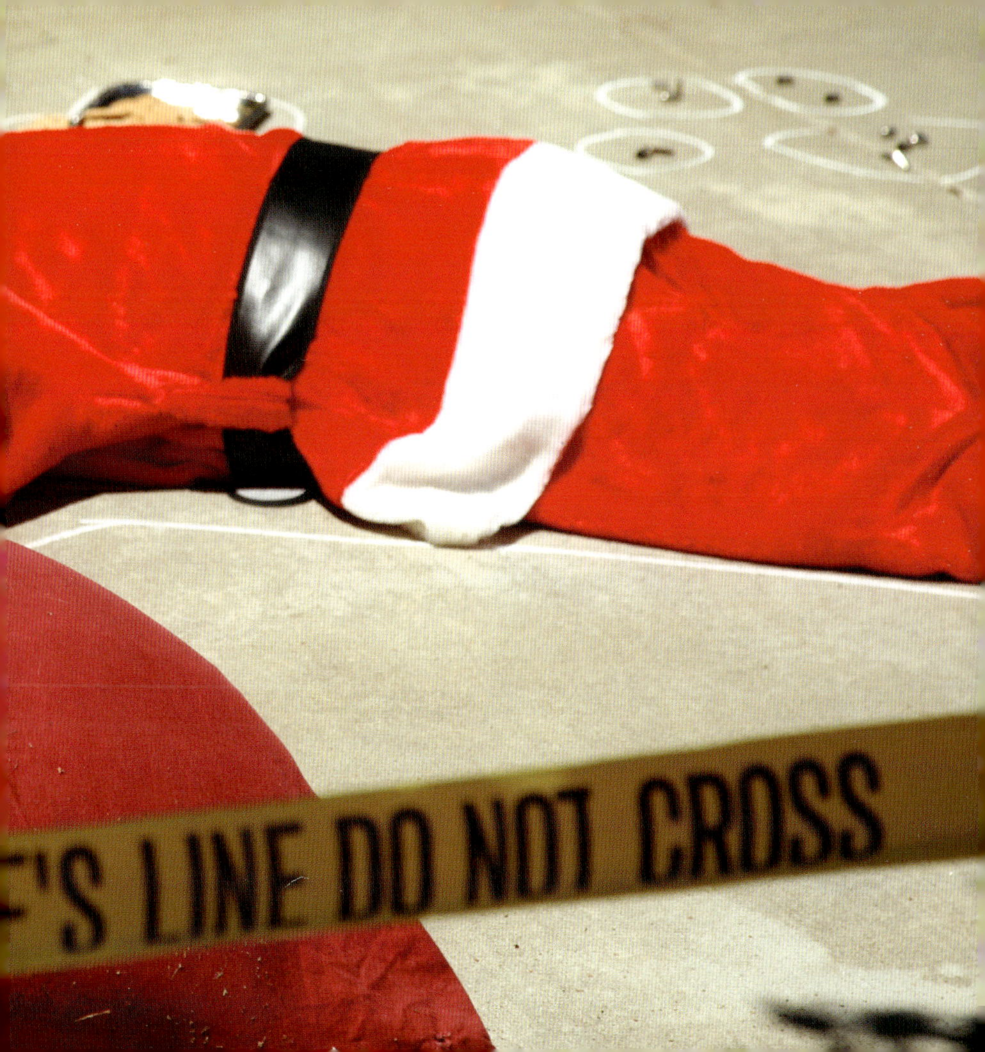
'S LINE DO NOT CROSS

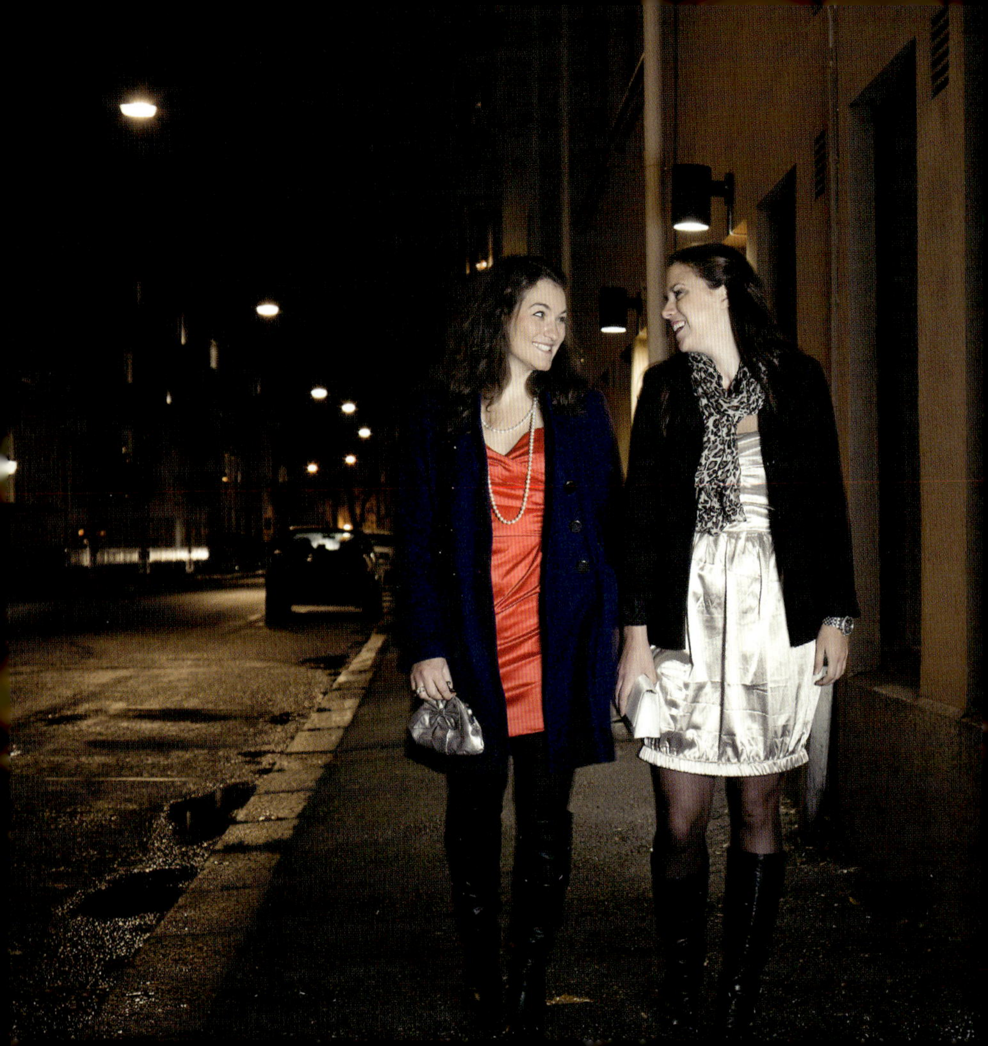

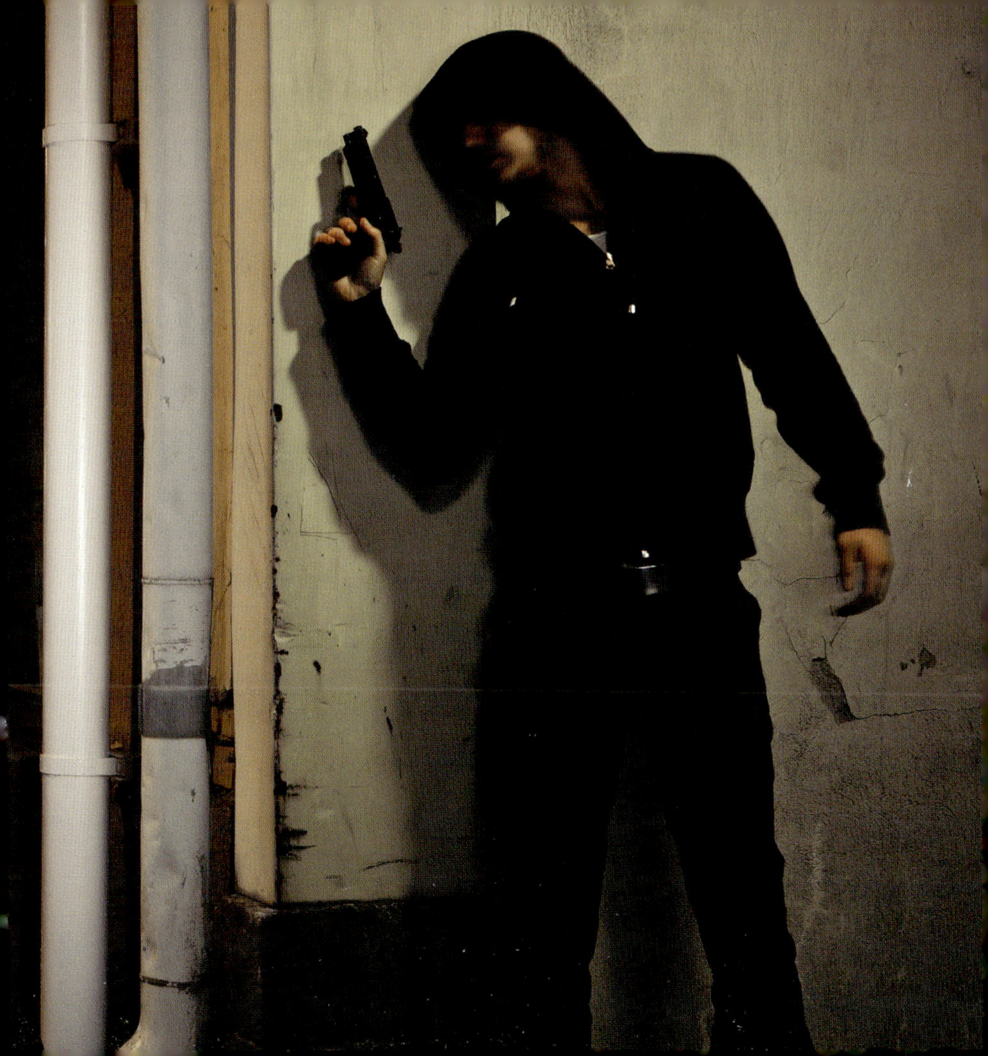

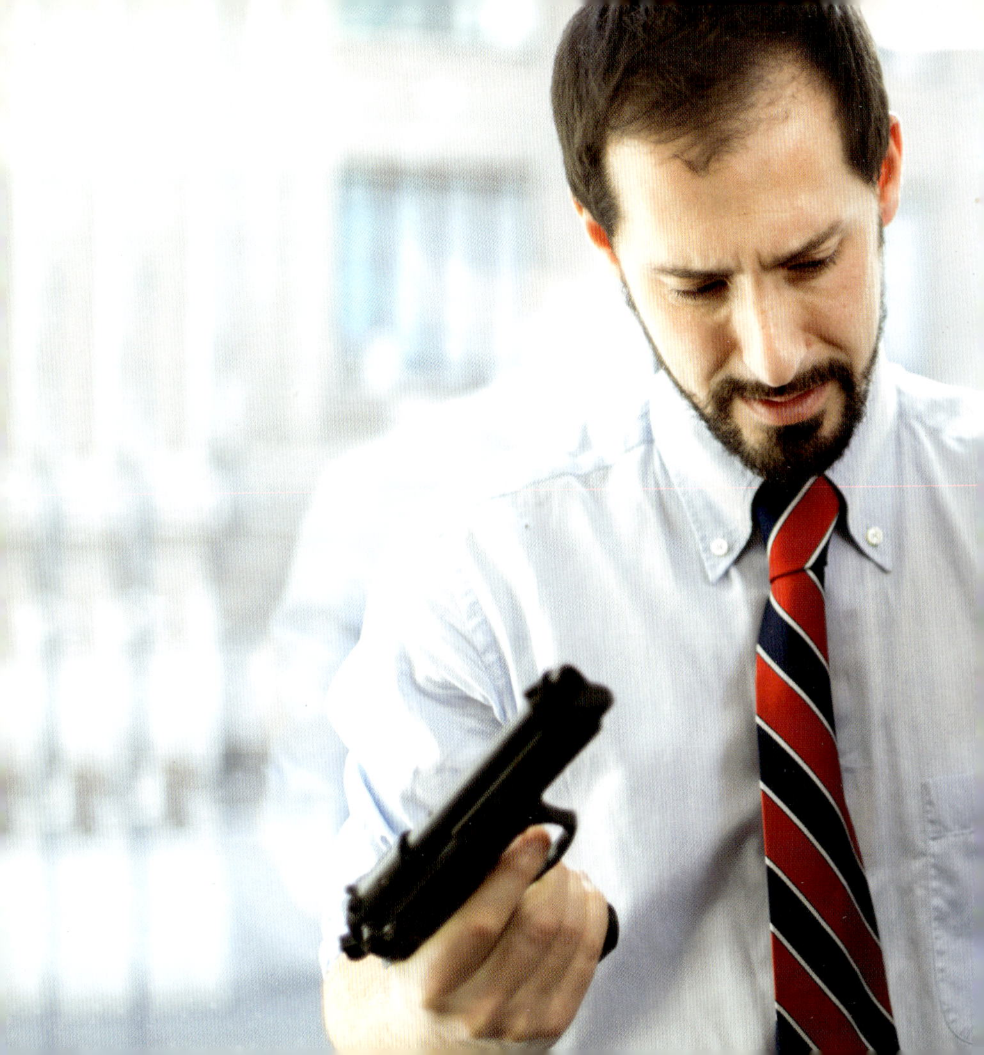

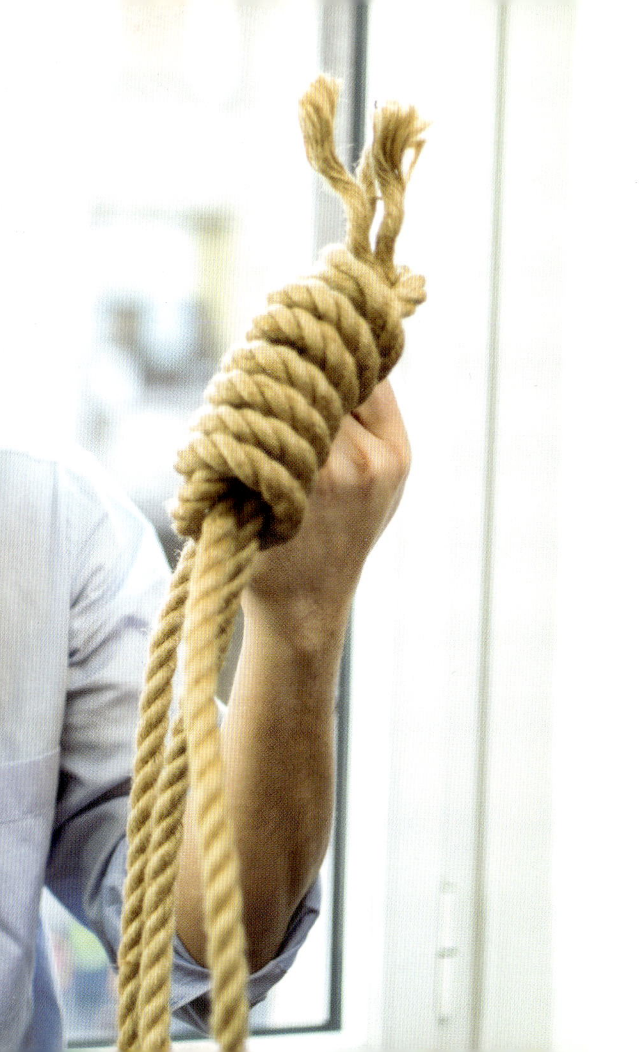

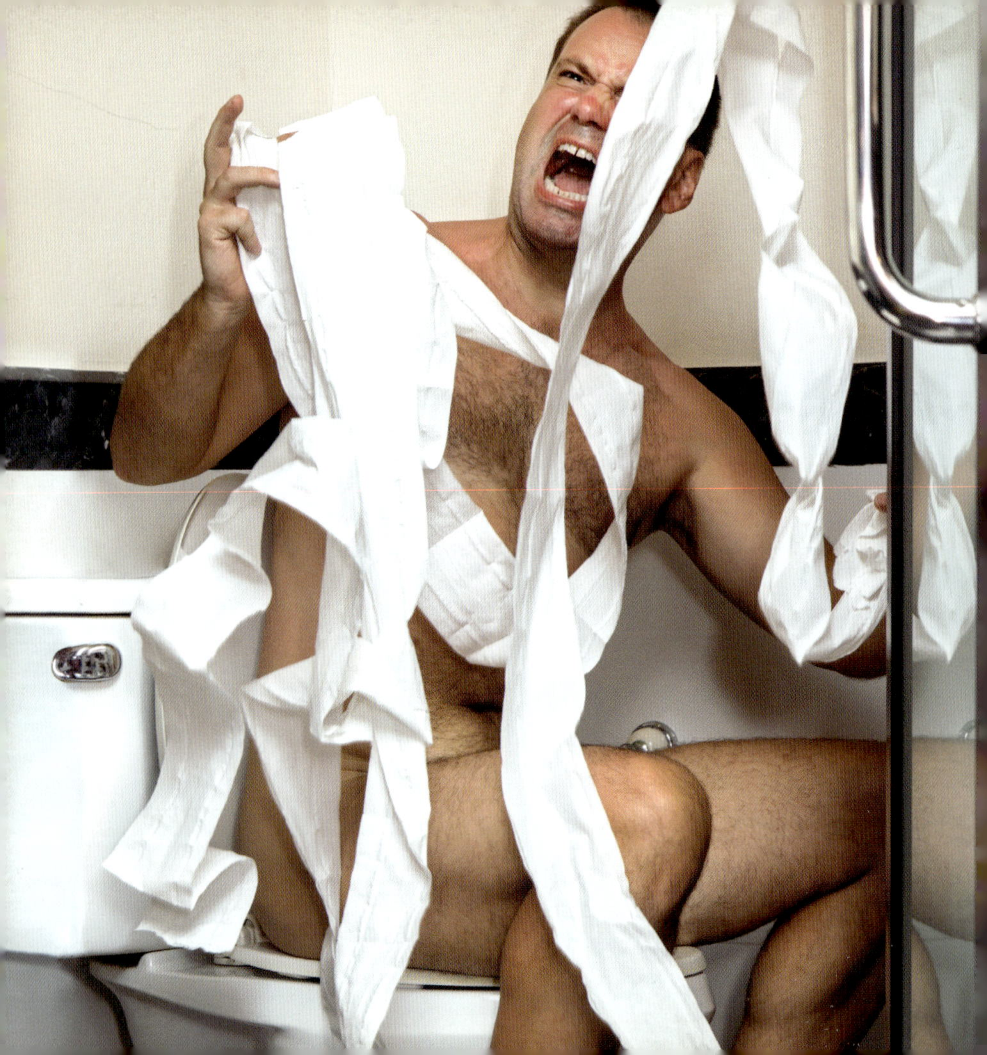

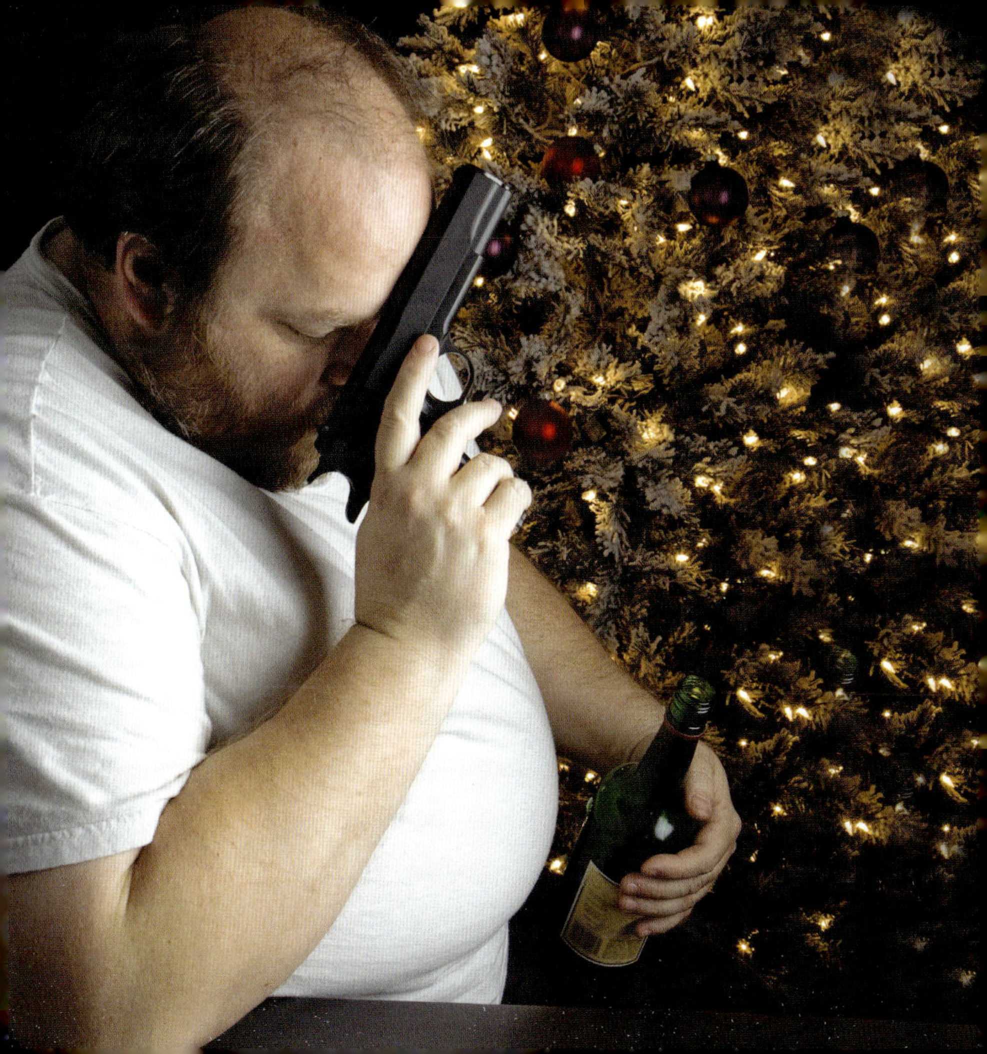

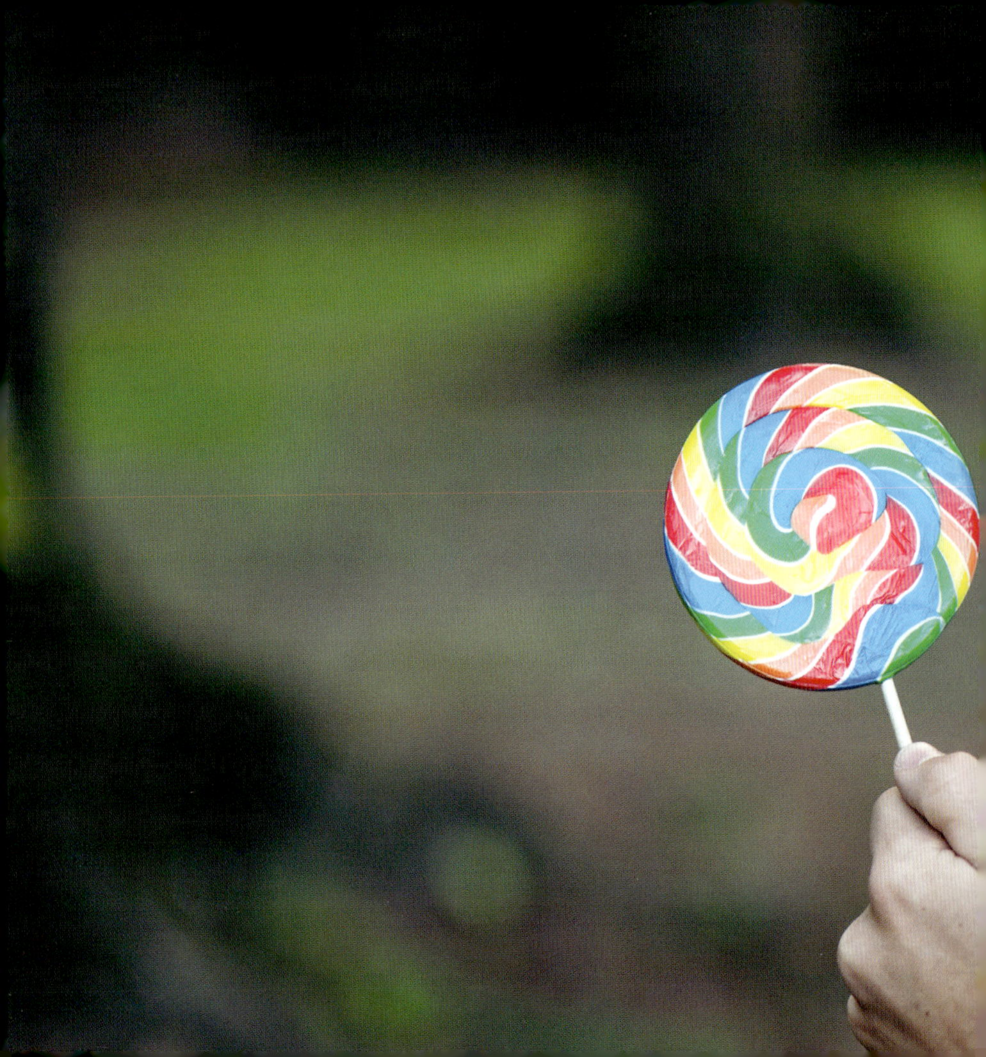

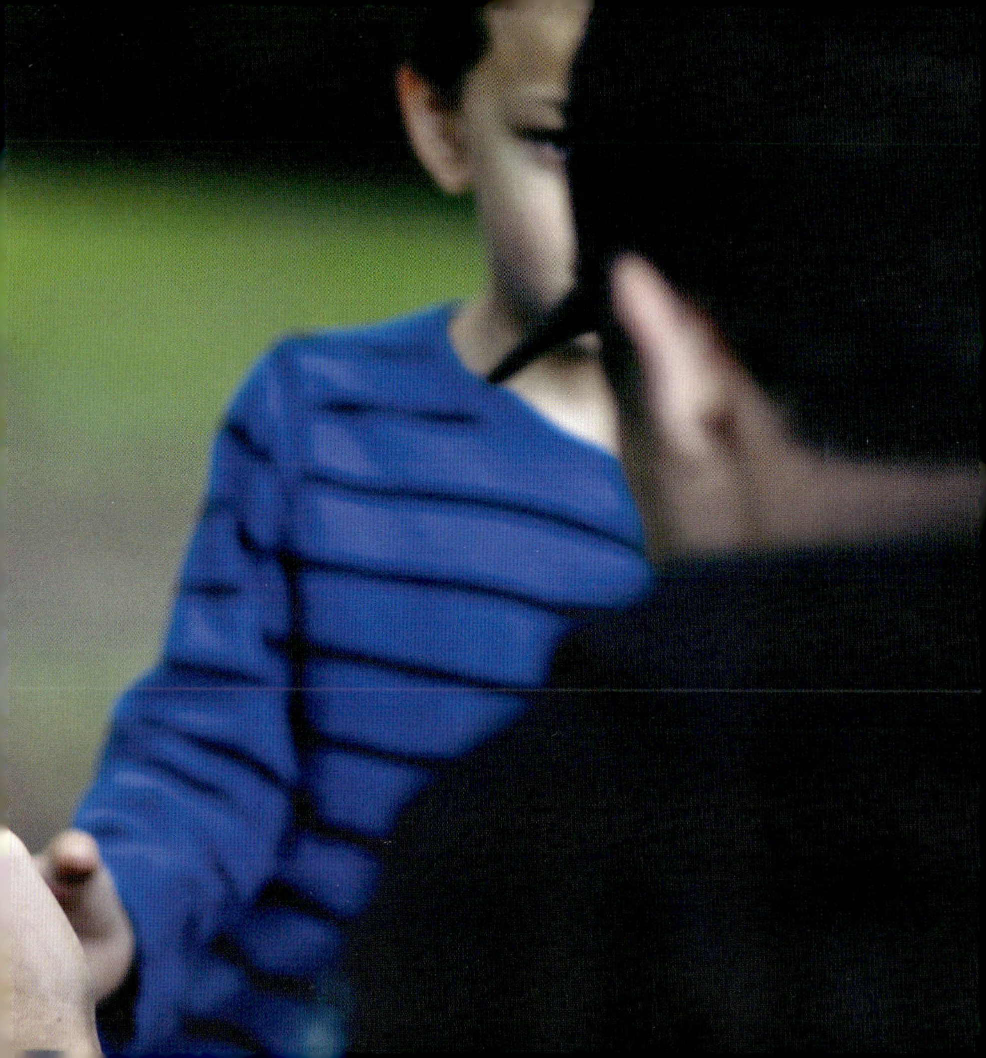

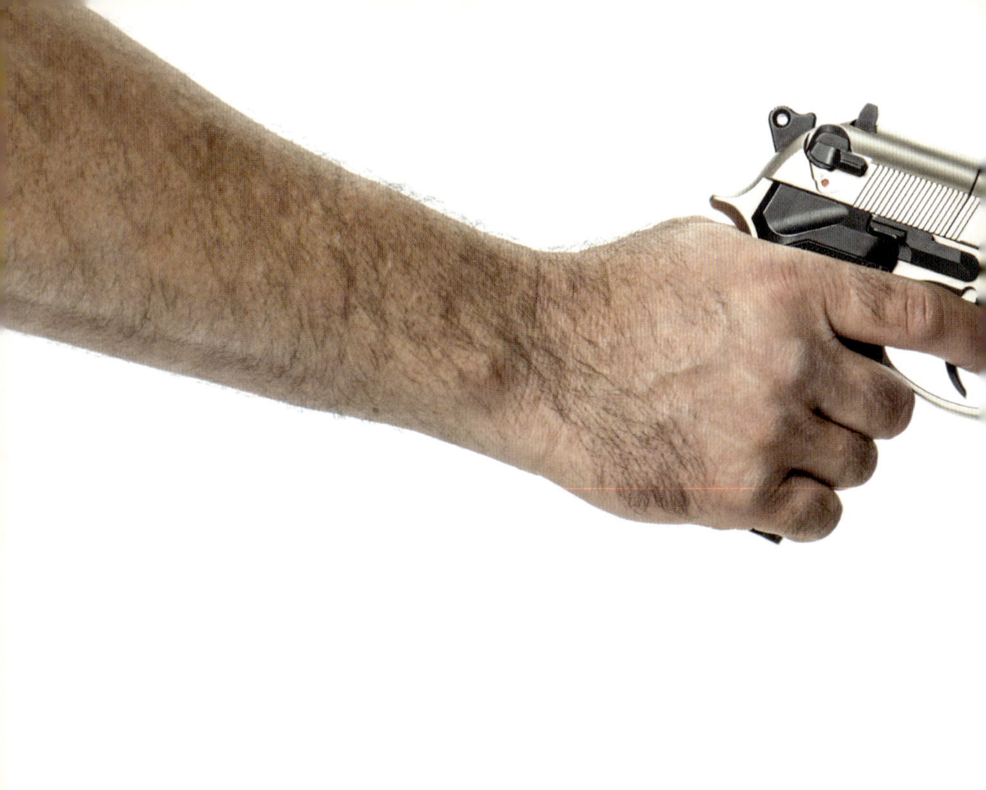

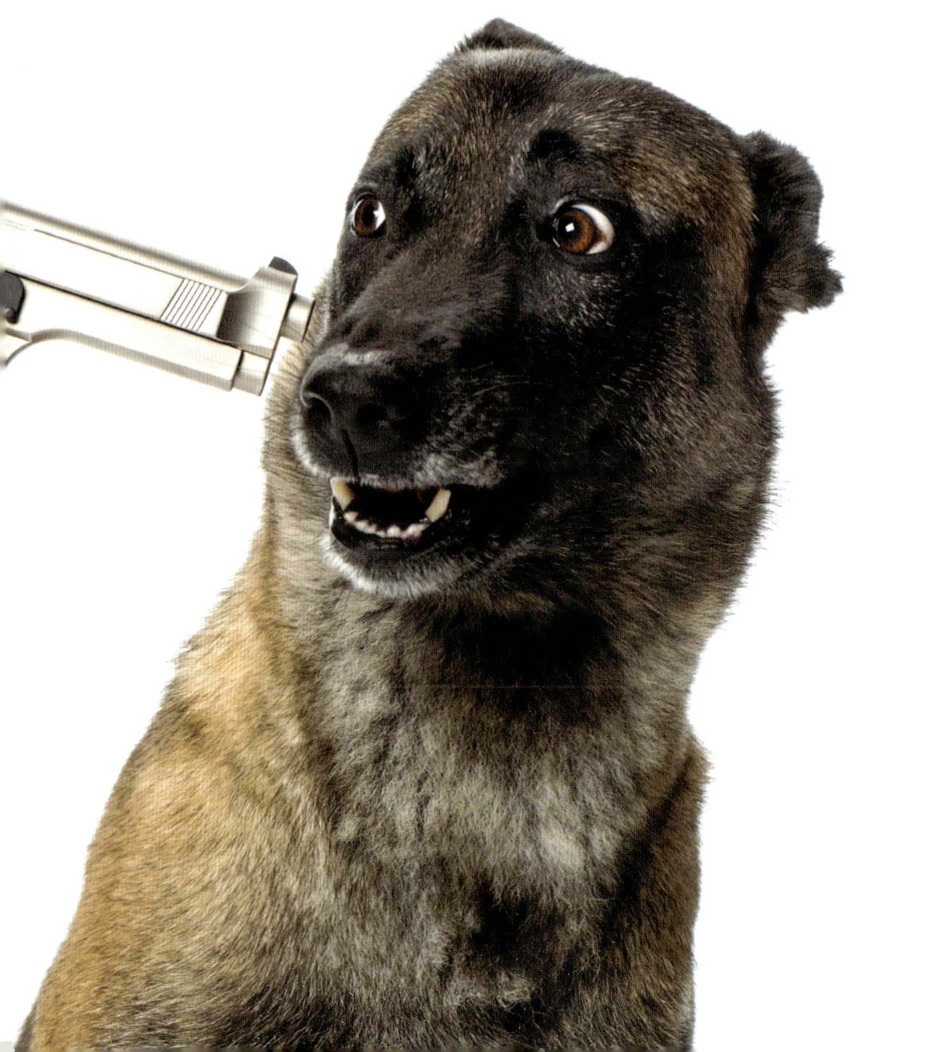

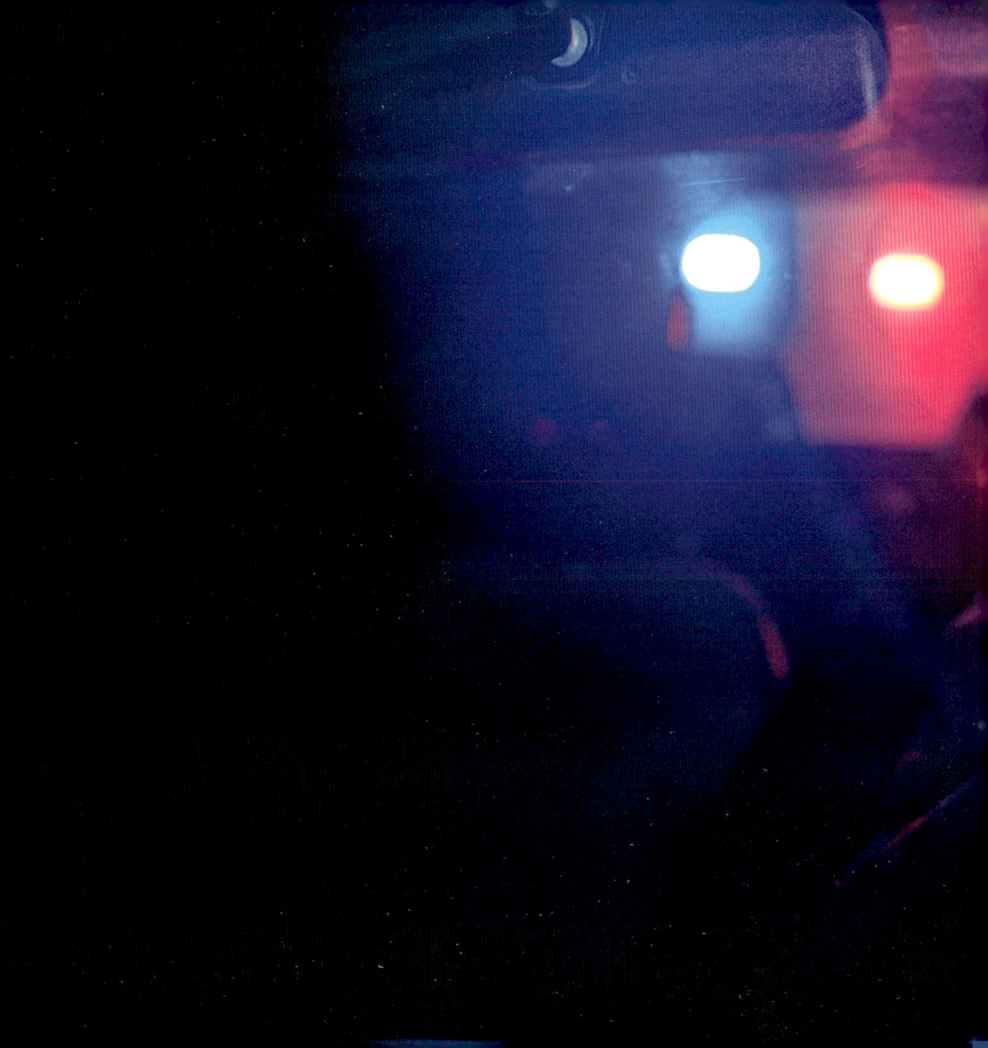

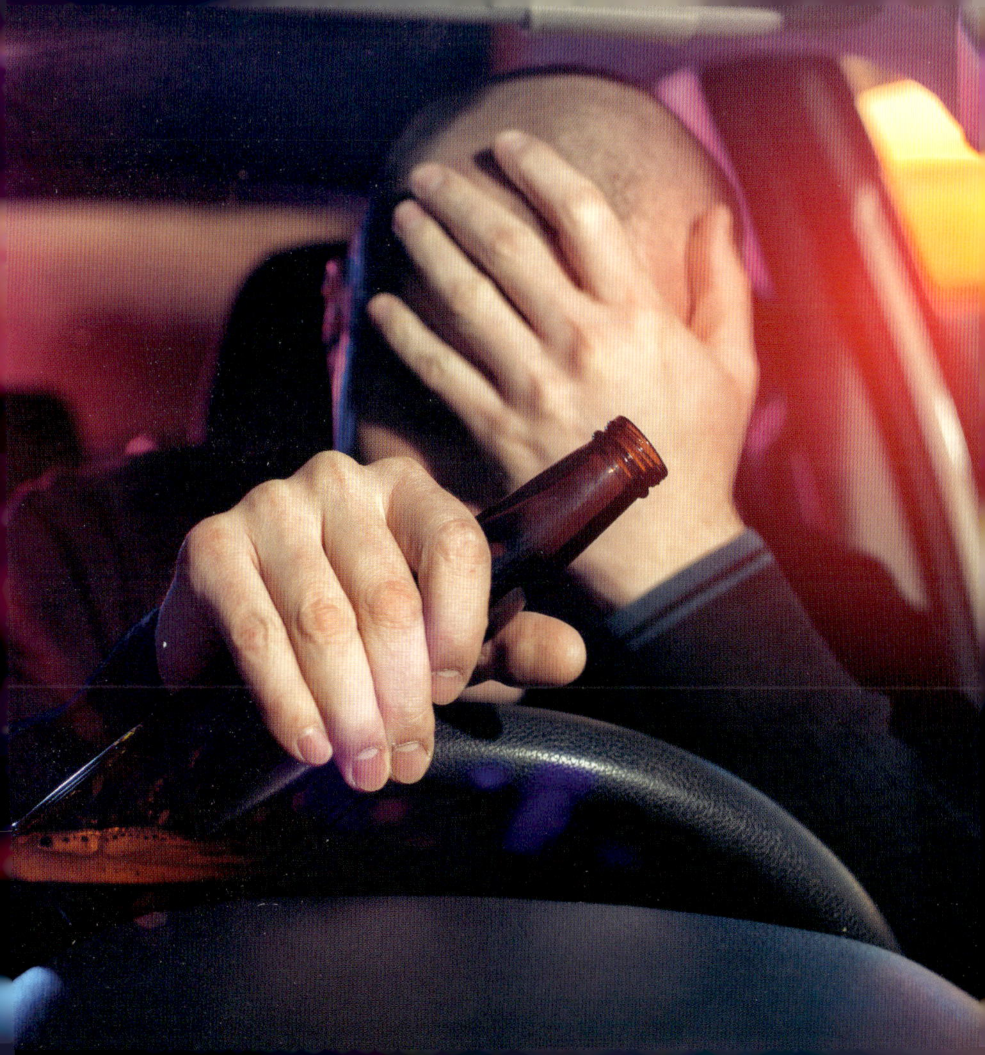

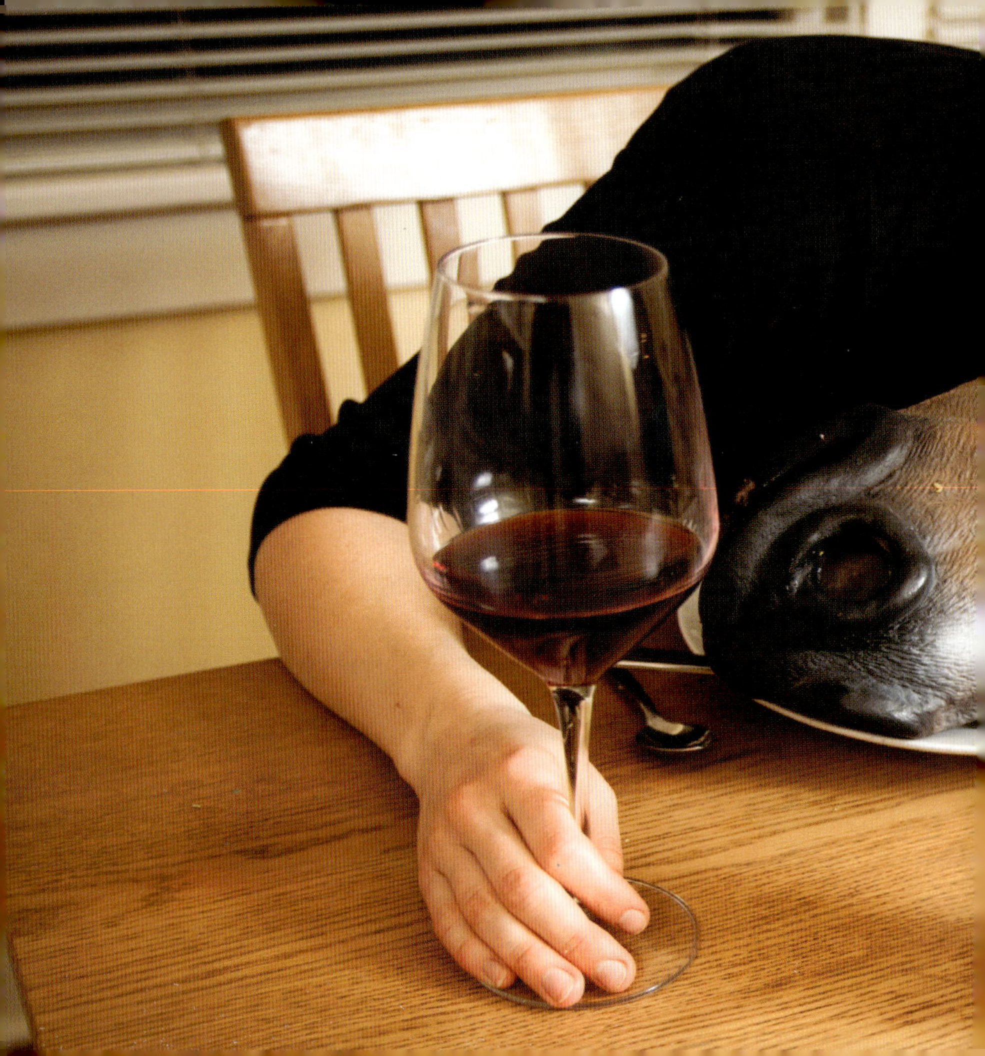

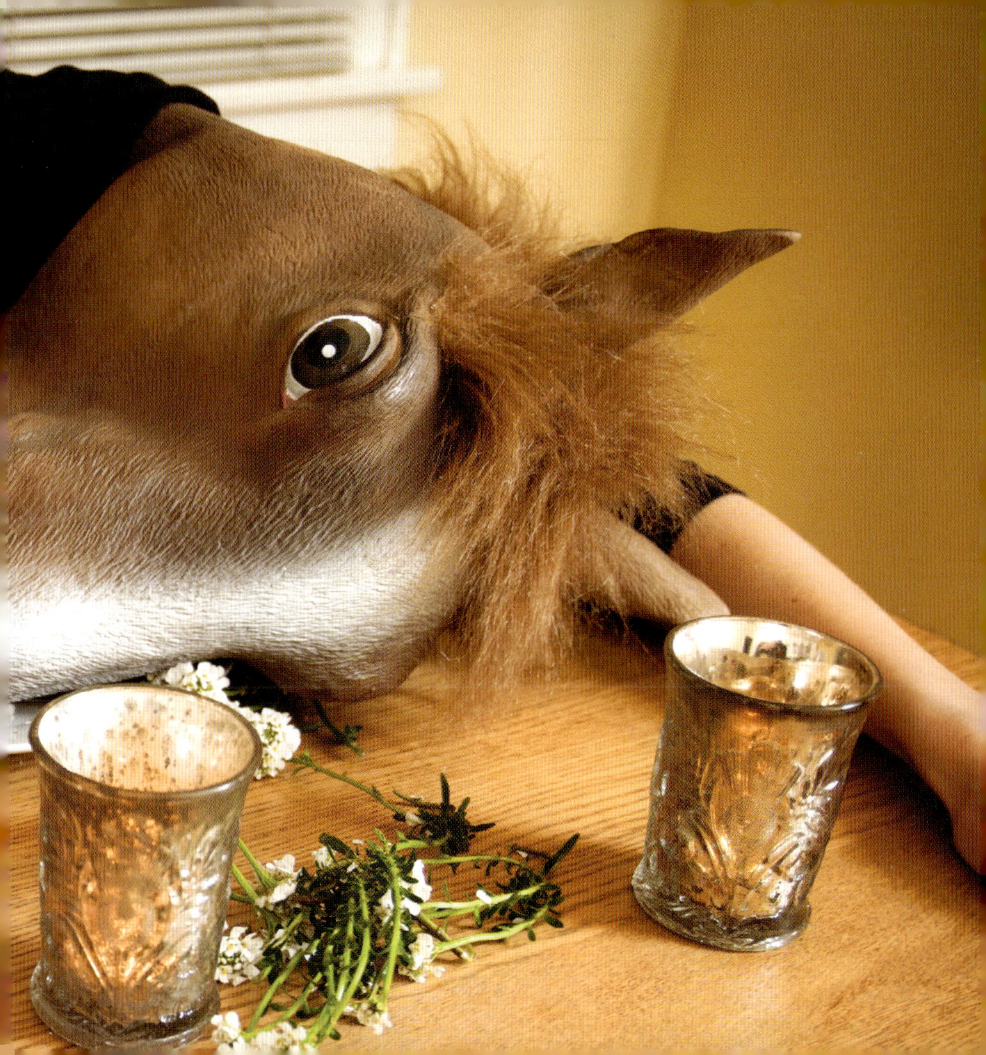

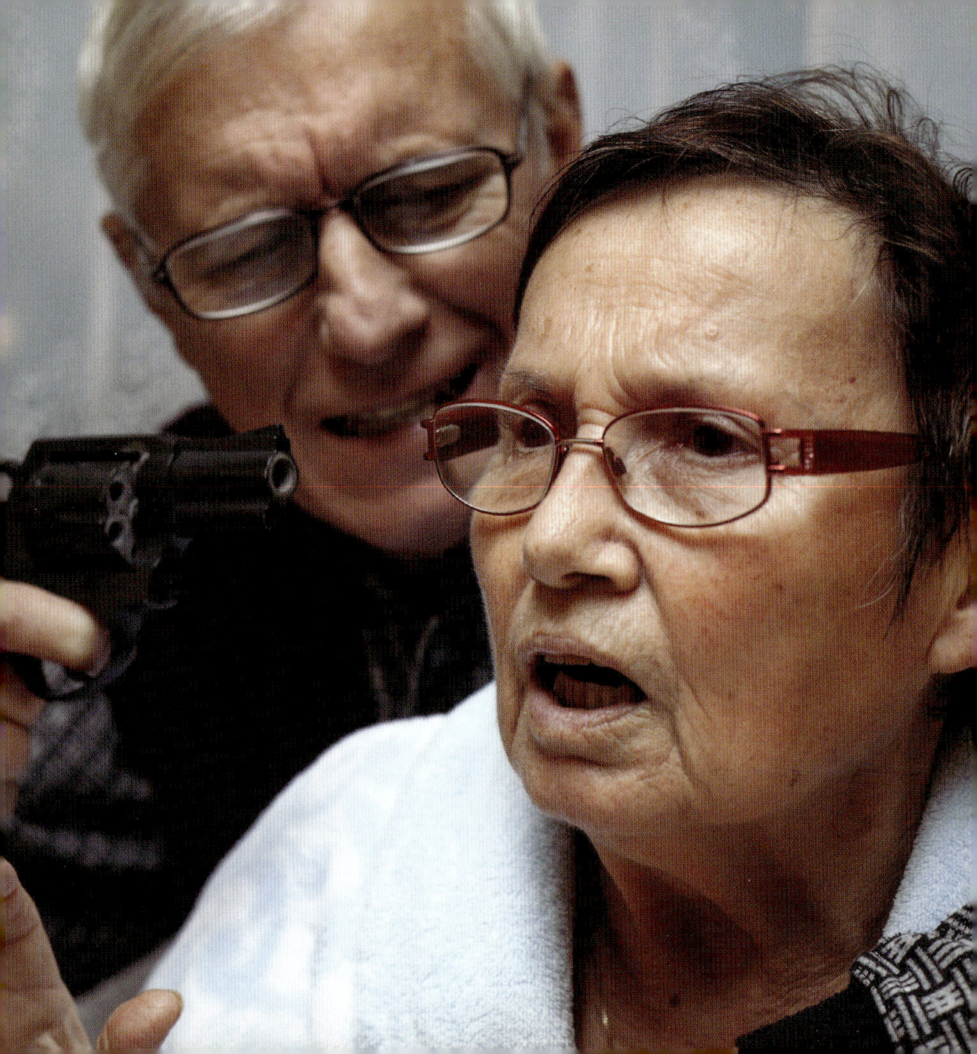

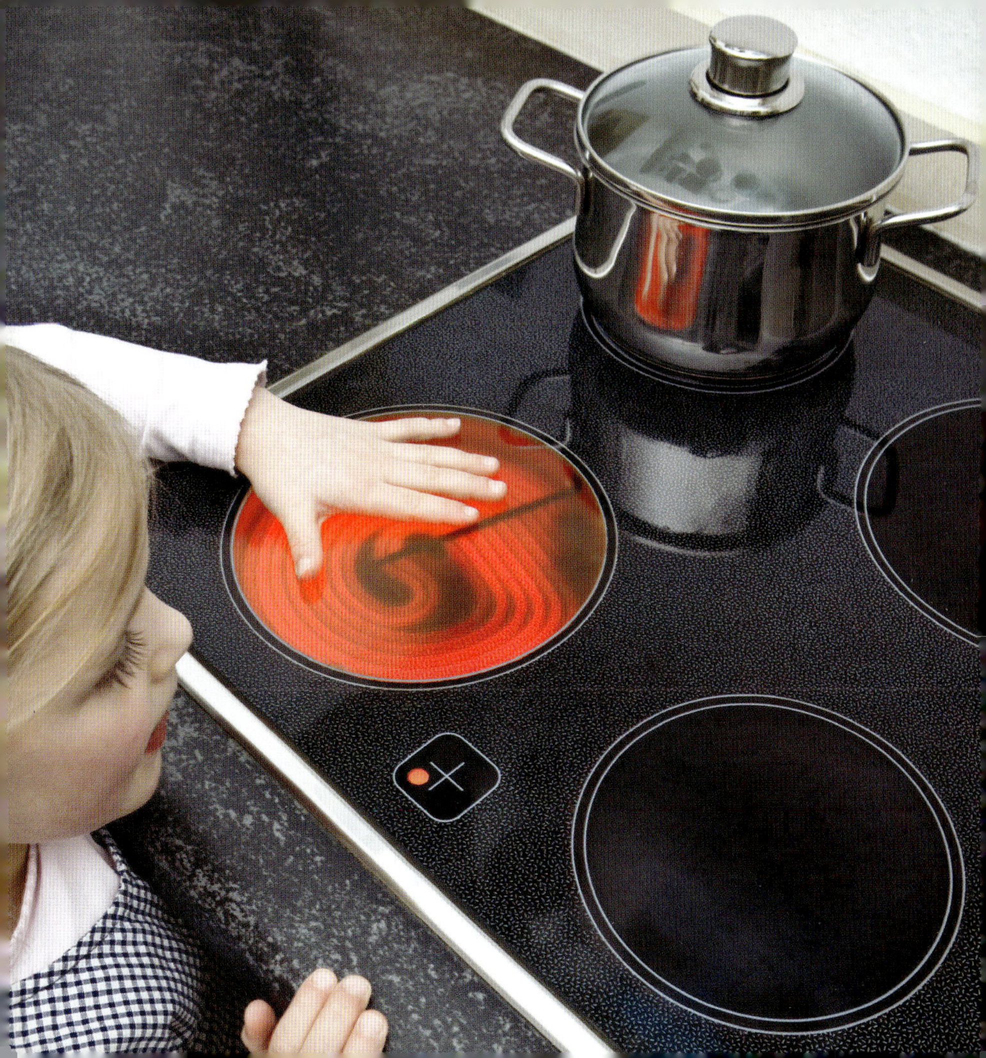

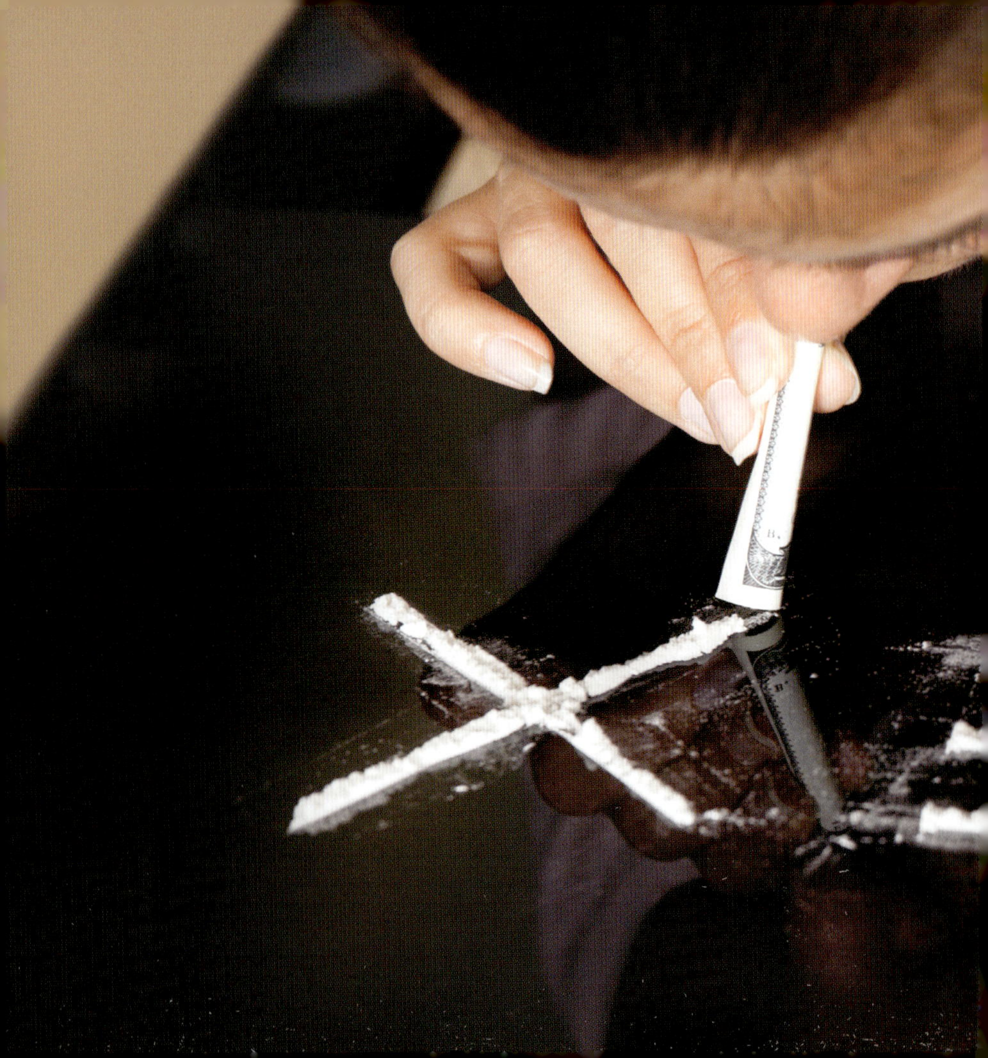

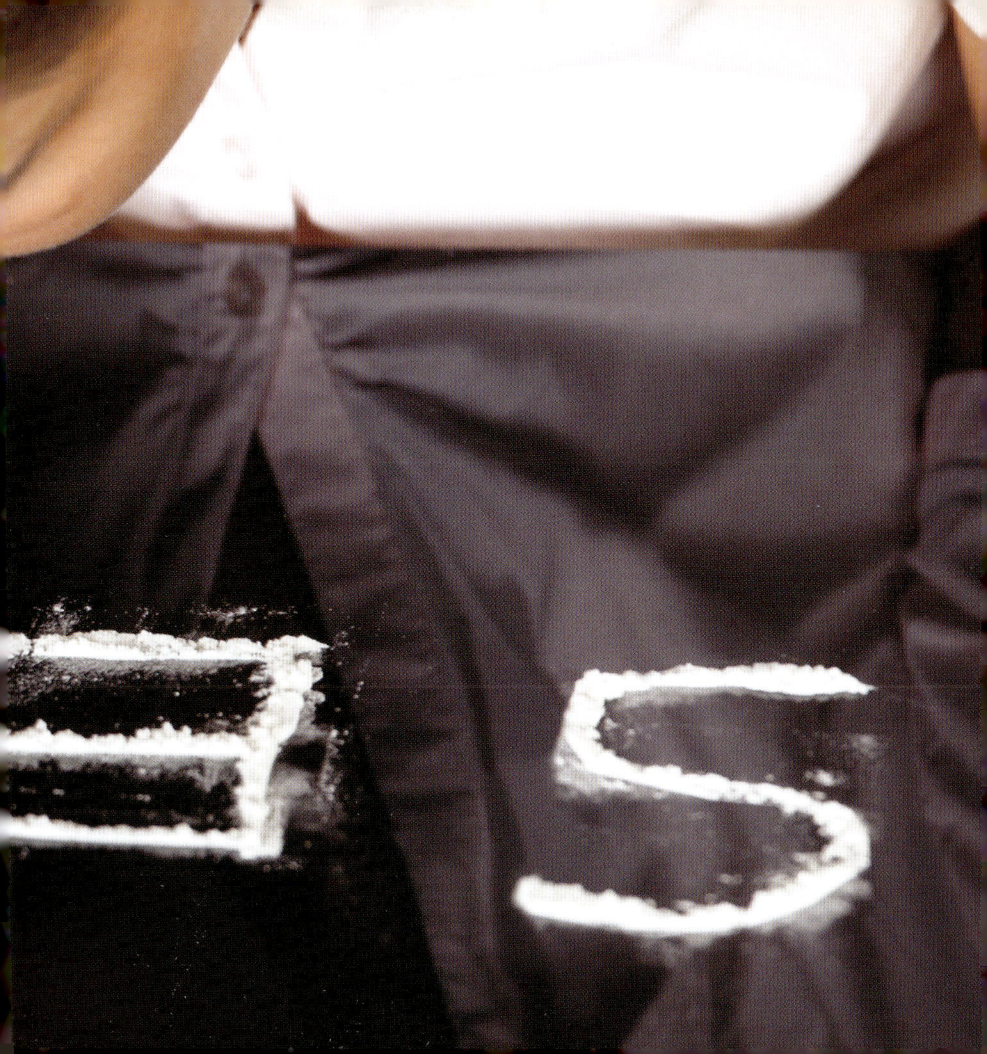

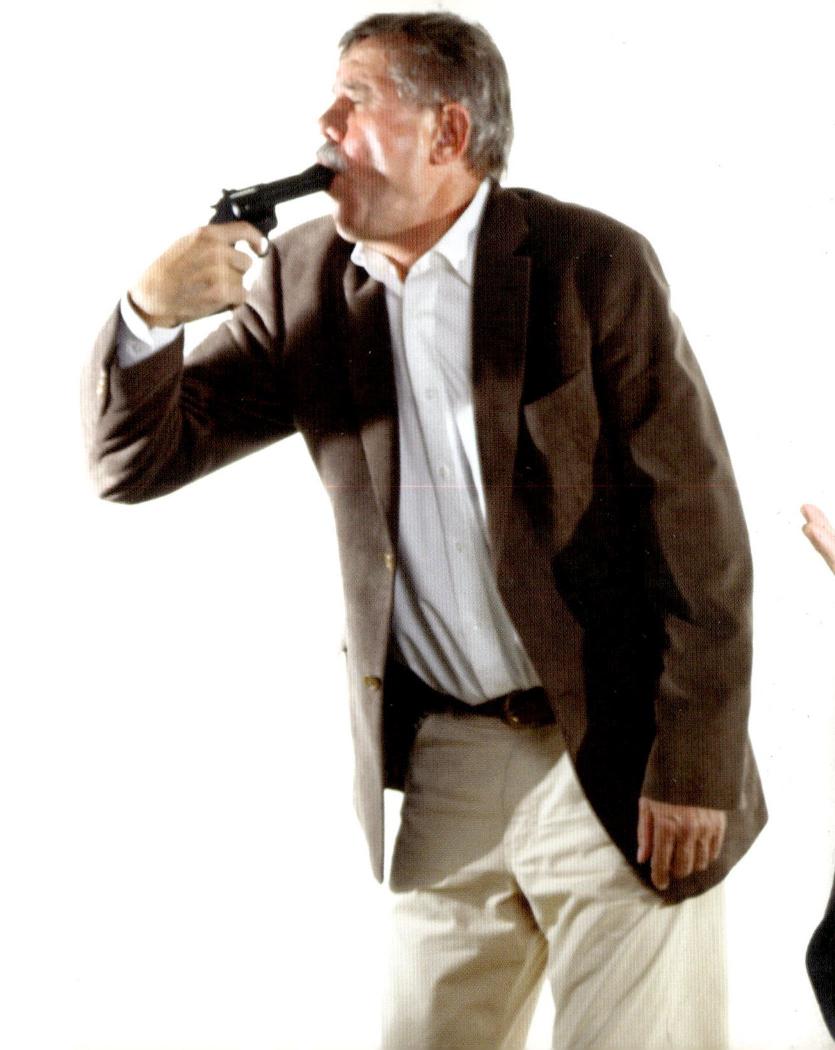

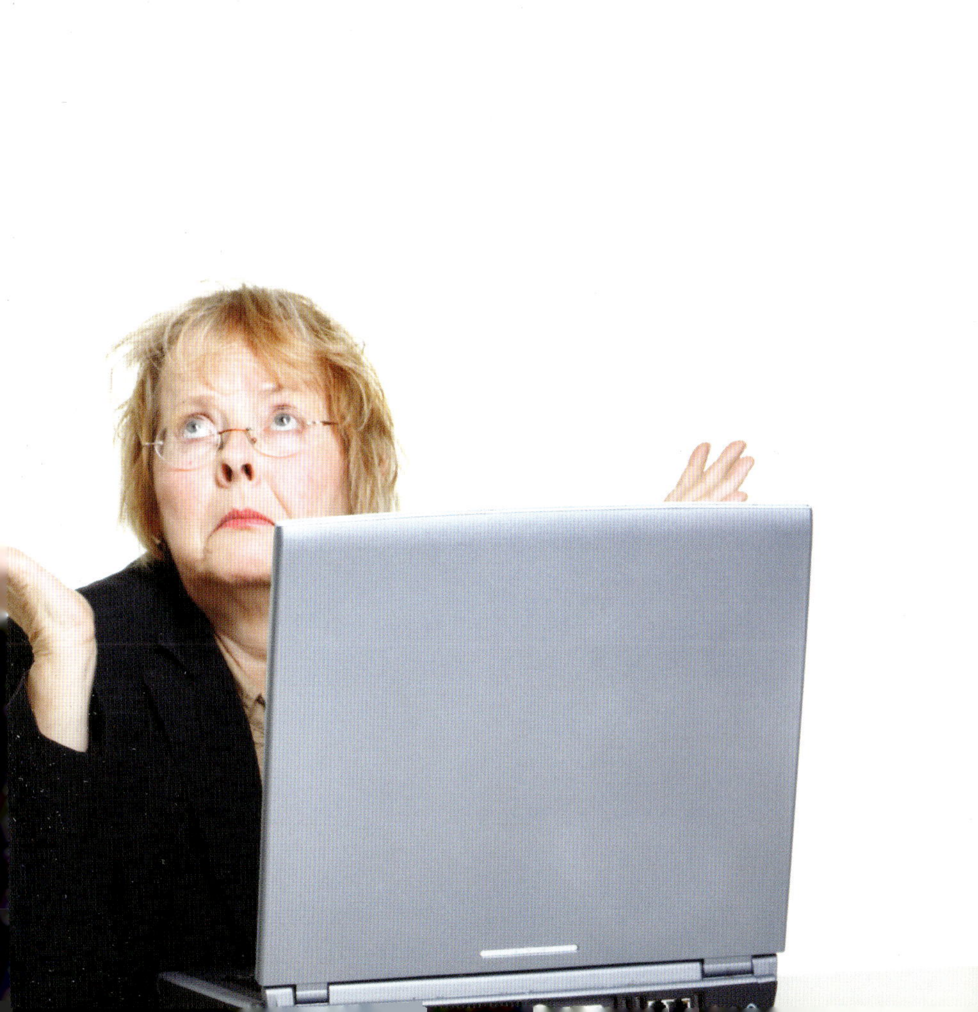

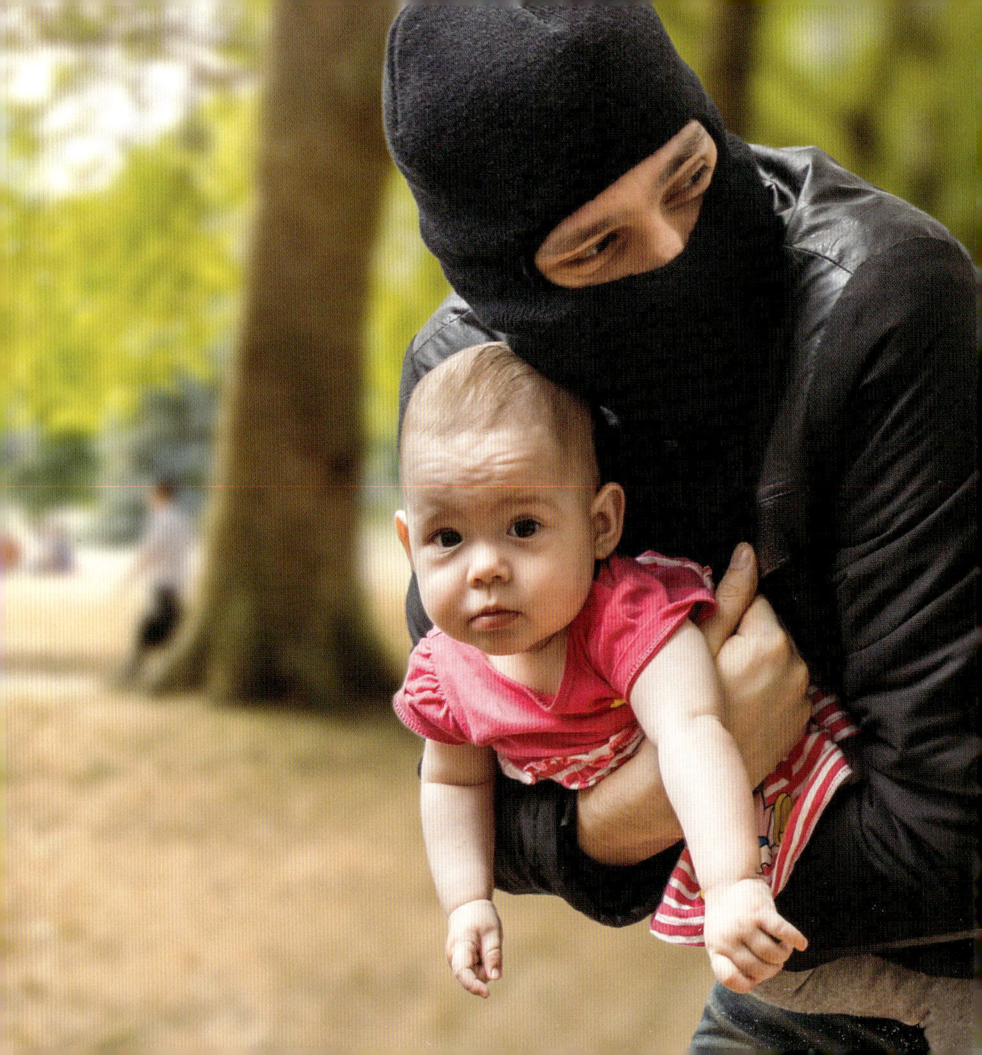

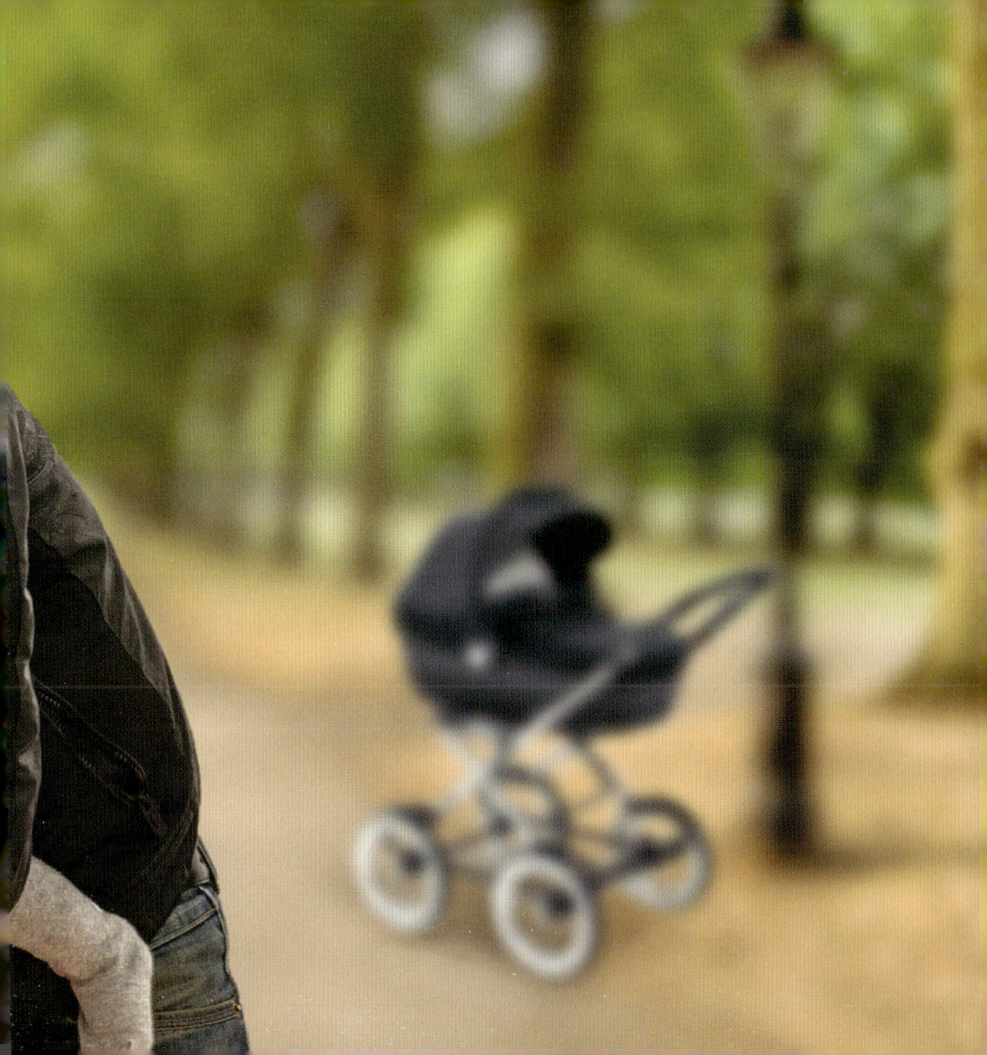

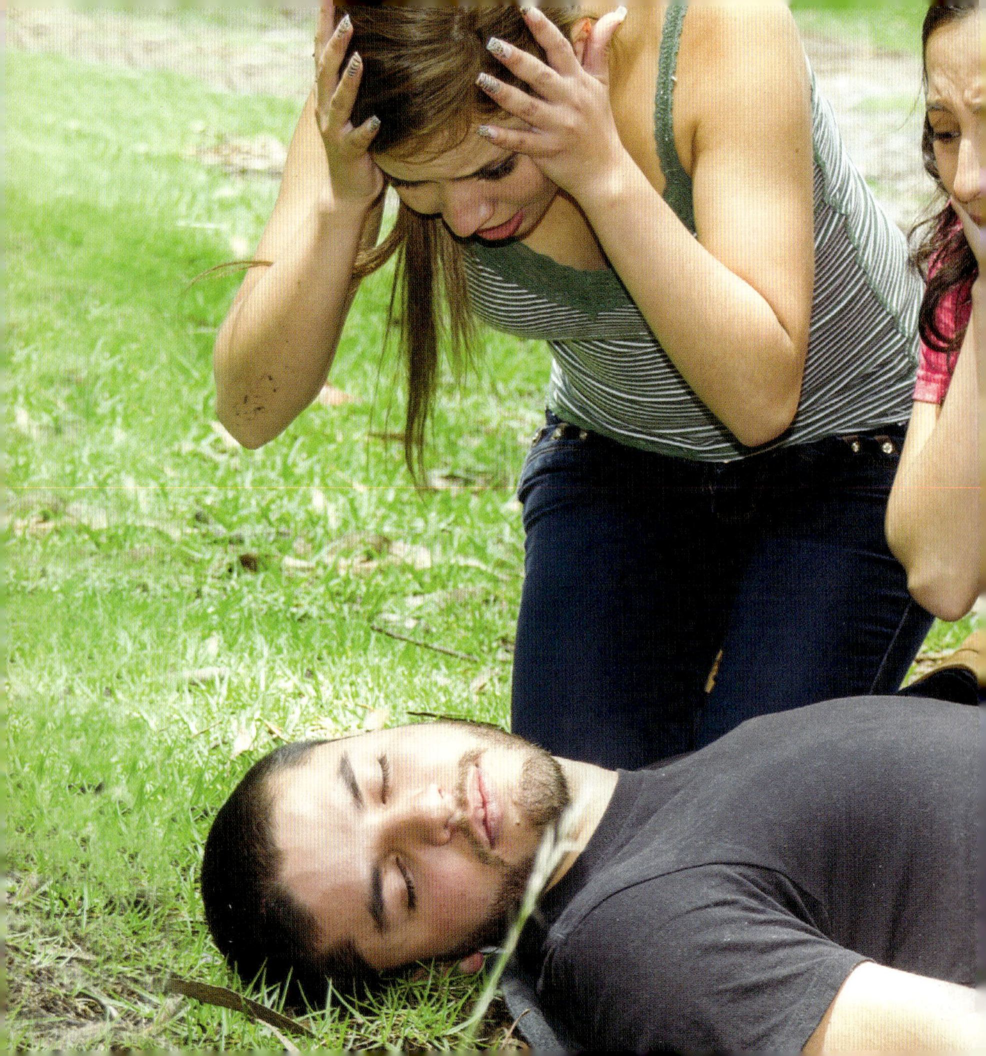

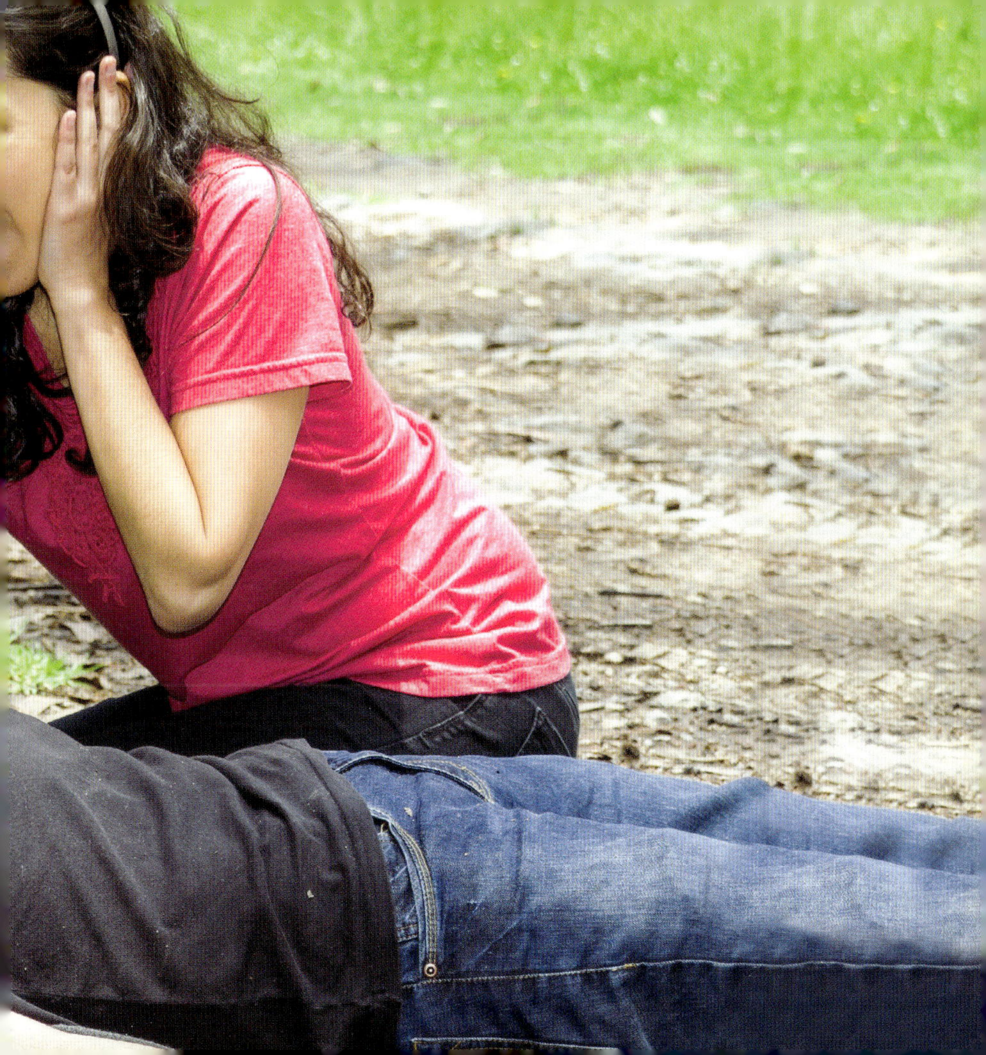

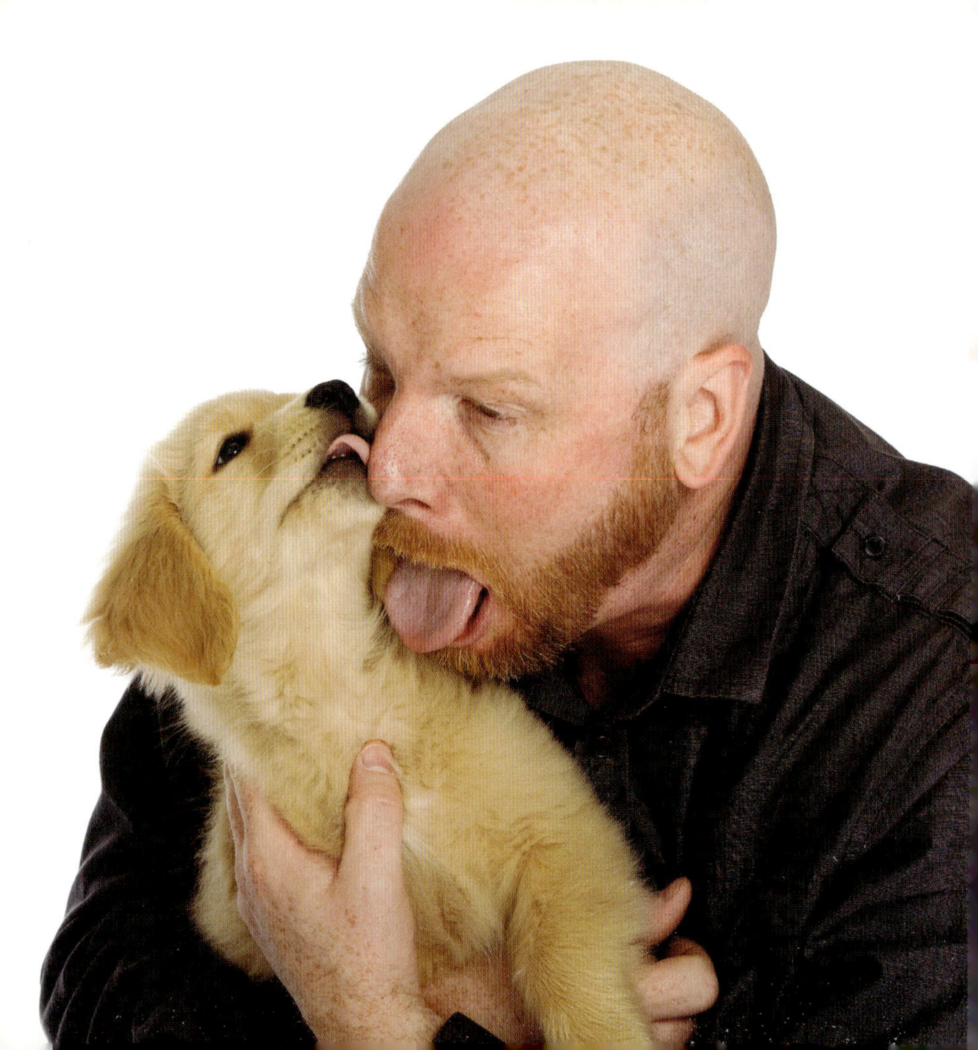

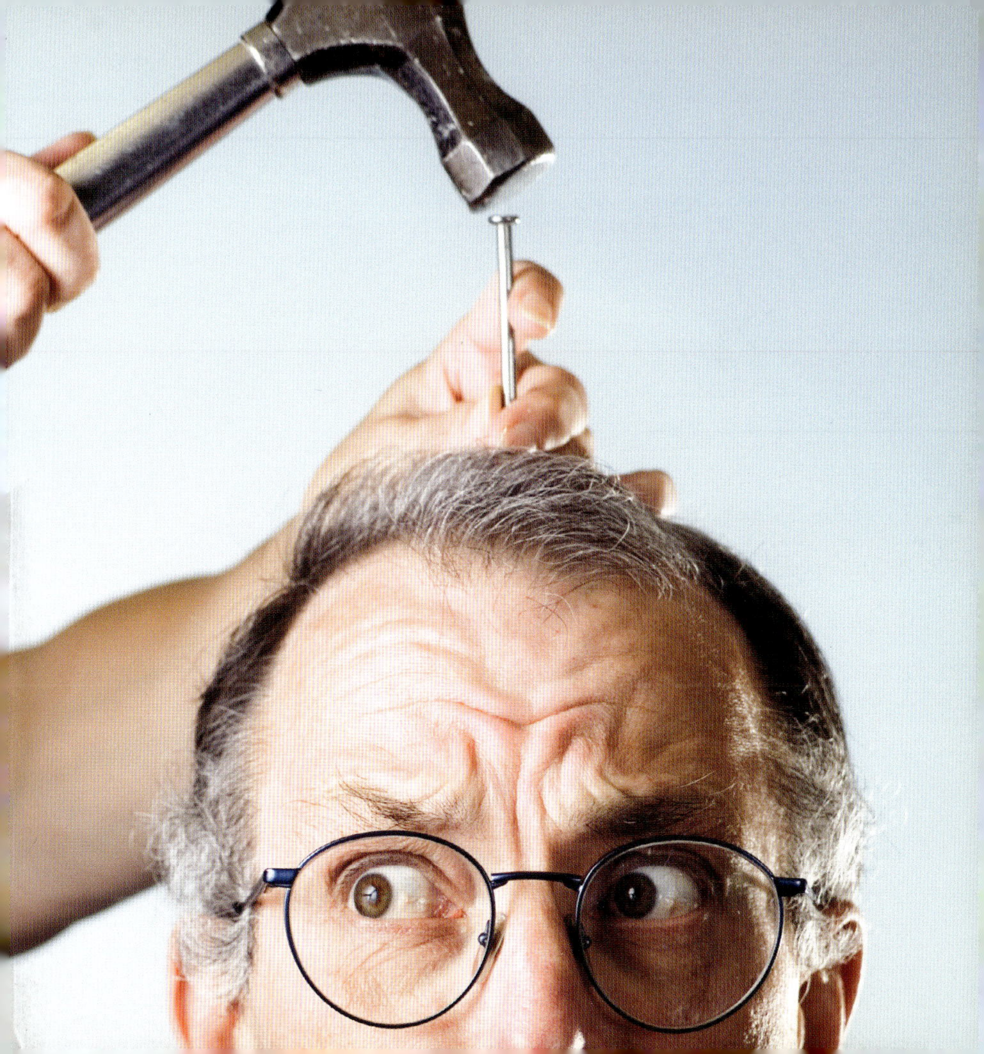

PICTURE CREDITS

123RF: Gilles DeCruyenaere, Lisa Young, Clinton L, Matthew Hayward, Andriy Popov, Ginasanders, Akz, Oleg Iandubaev

Depositphotos: Farina6000, JanMika, oneinchpunch, szefei, monkeybusiness, watman

Dreamstime: Matthias Ziegler, Milkovasa

Alamy: Jan Mika, Sunshine Pics, Kian Khoon Tan

Getty: hammerhead, Zero Creatives, RapidEye, nullplus, MichaelUtech, WilliamSherman, RichLegg, Alija, Richellgen, Yuri_Arcurs, 4x6, Vchal, FatCamera, CasarsaGuru

Shutterstock: Gilles DeCruyenaere, Lisa A., Mark Hayes, Monkey Business Images, CREATISTA, mikeledray, Gemenacom, Eric Isselee, Ambrozinio, Txking, Mangostock, Volodymyr Baleha, TFoxFoto, BlueSkyImage, Basileus, ChameleonsEye, komisar, Txking, Brian A Jackson, Jeff Thrower, Oksana Mizina, Lexxxx, Vchal, Paul Biryukov, File404, Minerva Studio, YAKOBCHUK VIACHESLAV, Elnur, Benevolente82, Milkovasa